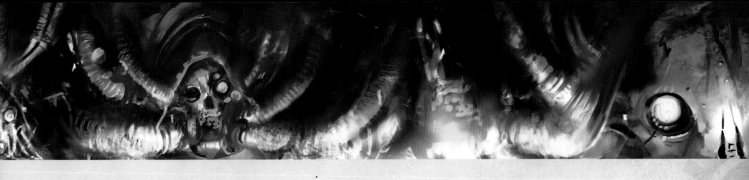

ADEPTUS MECHANICUS

WE KNOW EVERY FLEETING LIFEFORM IS A COG IN THE
GRAND MECHANISM. CAST OFF YOUR WEAK FLESH AND ACCEPT
THE GLORY OF THE MACHINE GOD. WE KNOW MORTAL FRAILTY
PALES BEFORE THE SECRETS REVEALED TO THE FAITHFUL,
AND WITH THE WISDOM OF CREATION AT OUR FINGERTIPS
THERE IS NO PRIZE BEYOND OUR ACQUISITION.
KNOWLEDGE IS ETERNAL.
KNOWLEDGE IS SACRED.
KNOWLEDGE IS POWER.

CONTENTS

PRODUCED BY THE WARHAMMER STUDIO

With thanks to the Mournival and the Infinity Circuit for their additional playtesting services

INTRODUCTION

Binharic blessings be upon you, devotee of the Machine God. The data contained within this holy tome will reveal the mysteries of the techno-religious cult of the Adeptus Mechanicus, and provide the means to command their cybernetic cohorts. Within these pages, you will learn of the ancient origins of this organisation, discover their industrial forge worlds and sacred iconography, and be provided with all the rules needed to field an army that can divine the secrets of the universe.

The Adeptus Mechanicus is amongst the most vital and powerful institutions within the Imperium, controlling the creation and use of Mankind's technology. Yet, woe to those who mistake these robed industrialists for mere fabricators or scientists. The ruling Tech-Priests of the Adeptus Mechanicus ferociously defend their monolithic manufactorums with legions of mechanically-augmented and devoted cybernetic warriors. Their armies also strike out into the dark galaxy, seeking lost archeotech and prying it from the grasp of those with lesser understanding. The Tech-Priests' strange engines of war rumble tirelessly over the battlefield, and their warriors carry weapons of ancient origin with which to unleash devastation. Robotic giants from before the dawn of the Imperium stomp over their enemies' defences, while a flickering chorus of binharic chants gives praise to the Machine God.

Collecting an Adeptus Mechanicus army puts their acquisitive zeal and bizarre technology at your command. Whether you are new to the hobby or a veteran Explorator, the tactics and creations of the Tech-Priests provide the tools to formulate the perfect battle plan. Volleys of radioactive slugs and electrical flares decimate foes at a distance, while predatory bio-mechanical warriors stalk the enemy, cutting them down with disruptive blades. Unthinking battle servitors – half-man and half-machine – obey their masters' imperatives without a second thought, disintegrating their opponents in burning plasma or ripping them asunder with gravitic forces. Charging cavalry mounted on canid cyborgs harry the flanks while airborne warriors fly overhead and into the fray.

The Adeptus Mechanicus range of miniatures comprises cowled warriors, machine-constructs and battle engines.

The detailed mechanisms and bionic limbs can be quickly and easily painted to a high standard with minimal effort, brought to life with simple techniques. Conversely, the wealth of detail and religious iconography affords expert painters the chance to lavish attention upon them, whether towards a grimy and industrial feel or pure and unsullied perfection.

Codex: Adeptus Mechanicus contains the history of this tech-savvy congregation, details of the politicking forge worlds it controls and its holy quest to acquire the universe's knowledge. Inside, you'll also find all the rules you need to turn your collection of miniatures into an unstoppable throng of holy artisans, featuring datasheets for every unit in the range, a collection of Warlord Traits and Relics, and tailored Crusade rules to precisely monitor your warriors' progress on their paths to greatness.

TO THE ADEPTUS MECHANICUS, DOUBT
IS AS ALIEN AS THE XENOS HORRORS
THAT ASSAIL MANKIND'S REALM. WHEN
THE RULING CABALS OF HOODED AND
BIONICALLY AUGMENTED TECH-PRIESTS
COMMIT THEIR VAST ARMIES TO BATTLE,
THEY HAVE ALREADY ENUMERATED EVERY
PARAMETER. EACH VARIABLE HAS BEEN
MEASURED AND ASSIGNED A PROBABILITY
MATRIX. ALL THAT REMAINS IS TO EXECUTE
THE PROTOCOLS OF WAR, WHICH ARE
HANDED DOWN TO THE PRIESTHOOD'S SEMI-
MECHANICAL FOLLOWERS AS DIVINE SIGNS,
UNDENIABLE PROOFS OF THE MACHINE GOD'S
POWER. TO FACE THE ADEPTUS MECHANICUS
IS TO OPPOSE THOSE WHO HAVE ALREADY
CALCULATED YOUR DEMISE.

FROM THEIR SOVEREIGN HOLDINGS ON
INDUSTRY-CHOKED AND SMOG-WREATHED
FORGE WORLDS, THE ADEPTUS MECHANICUS
REACH OUT TO SCOUR THE DIM REACHES
OF THE GALAXY FOR FORGOTTEN FRAGMENTS
OF ARCHEOTECH FROM MANKIND'S PAST.
THEIR RULERS ARE FANATICALLY ZEALOUS,
RIGIDLY DOGMATIC AND REVERE TECHNOLOGY
AS THE OBJECT OF THEIR DEVOTIONS. YET
TRUE UNDERSTANDING OF THE ARTEFACTS
THEY SEEK EVER GIVES WAY TO A GREATER
PRINCIPLE: WORSHIP OF THEIR MACHINE
GOD, WHO INVESTS CREATIONS WITH
THE MOTIVE FORCE. VERBAL PROTOCOLS
HAVE DEVOLVED INTO MURMURED CHANTS,
RIGOROUS THEOREMS INTO RELIGIOUS
DOCTRINE AND TECHNOLOGICAL REVOLUTION
INTO STULTIFYING INERTIA.

THEY ASPIRE TO THE PURITY OF THE
MACHINE, BUT THE ADEPTUS MECHANICUS
RETAIN ALL THE FERVENT FAITH AND
OBSESSIVE AMBITION OF THEIR HUMANITY.

DISCIPLES OF THE MACHINE GOD

The Adeptus Mechanicus are the custodians of Mankind's technological knowledge. With great reverence and elaborate ritual, robed priests oversee the fabrication, maintenance and repair of every device crafted by Mankind, and view the careful protection of every scrap of ancient information as their religious duty.

The Adeptus Mechanicus – its complex hierarchies of ruling Tech-Priests and their myriad followers – devote themselves to the divine trinity of the Machine God, the Omnissiah and the Motive Force: the source of all knowledge, the embodiment of wisdom and the animus that empowers all. In their eyes, technology and the act of its creation are sacred concepts worthy of adoration, while the corruption of these ideals is heresy that invites condemnation and death. Mankind's technology is ancient. Much of it dates back to the dark time of legend before the Imperium, and it is through the Tech-Priests' religion – the Cult Mechanicus – that Humanity still retains fragments of this knowledge. The faith of the Cult Mechanicus is founded on dogma and rote, repeated maniacally without change over more than ten thousand years, while true understanding of many of their practices has long since vanished under a smothering blanket of ritual and half-remembered mummery. Priests soothe the intractable machine spirits of cogitators, reignite the fiery hearts of recalcitrant generatoria and forge the materiel used by the Imperium's armies as much with sprays of holy incense and binharic chants as with technical skill. To the Adeptus Mechanicus, the production and maintenance of the machine is indivisible from their theology, and even the most mundane process is performed with all the ceremony of a rite millennia in its practice. Tech-Priests declaim the hand of the Machine God in every aspect of Human technology, in the fundamental forces of the universe and in their own ability to comprehend such divine concepts.

Such knowledge is precious, and the Adeptus Mechanicus jealously guard their power and influence in a carefully choreographed balance with the Imperium's other great powers. Without the forges and specialist knowledge of the Tech-Priests – however fragmented and ill-used – the Imperium would swiftly fall; and without the incomprehensibly vast resources and military might of the rest of the Imperium, the Adeptus Mechanicus would crumble and vanish. Both benefit hugely from a sometimes strained yet irrevocably connected dependence.

WORKS OF DIVINITY
Through the sweat of legions of slave labour, the augmented strength of unthinking cyborg thralls and the power of monolithic forge temples do the Adeptus Mechanicus create everything from pioneer ploughshares to Ramilies class star forts. Simple black powder explosives in use on feudal mining worlds, hololithic strategium projectors, manufactorums bigger than city-states and God-Engines that can level such conglomerations in a single, apocalyptic salvo – all fall under the auspices of the Adeptus Mechanicus. Through ancient covenants with the Emperor himself, the adepts of the Cult Mechanicus have a monopoly on and jurisdiction over the use of all technology. To alter a machine's prescribed operation or structure, to interfere with its inner workings without the proper theological ministrations only a Tech-Priest is privy to, are just some of the crimes for which the Adeptus Mechanicus is privileged to administer punishment. Lobotomised servitors – men and women who ran afoul of the Tech-Priests – are a common sight throughout the Imperium. These unthinking creatures, heavily modified with bionic replacements, perform menial and repetitive tasks of every kind, and their unhealthy pallor and slack jaws are a potent reminder of the dangers of crossing the Adeptus Mechanicus.

COHORTS AND LEGIOS
The Tech-Priests do not exert their influence solely by their integration in the Imperium's other institutions. The Adeptus Mechanicus retains the right to raise standing armies of its own. Their ranks are the iron fist that both enforces the Tech-Priests laws and defends the sacred forge worlds that are the hubs of their rulers' domains. They also project the Adeptus Mechanicus' power out into the galaxy on pious quests to unearth traces of Humanity's technological legacy.

The numberless cohorts of the Skitarii Legions are the cybernetic heart of the Tech-Priests' military might. They are the foot soldiers of the Cult Mechanicus, fully devoted to the faith, and heavily modified by their masters with bionic enhancements, their neural cortexes inloaded with martial protocols. To witness them marching to war is akin to seeing a bizarre and grotesque religious procession conducted with scientific precision. They are a macabre mix of the living tissue and mechanical augmentation, responding immediately to the broadcast imperatives of their superiors.

The Skitarii do not crusade alone in the name of the Machine God. The hulking automatons of the Legio Cybernetica crush the unwary beneath their tread and stitch incandescent trails of burning phosphor through the enemy ranks. The Centurio Ordinatus marshal leviathan war machines that each bear unique and irreplaceable munitions of incredible power. The Ordo Reductor specialise in siege warfare and worship the Machine God in its aspect as the un-maker, the Auxilia Myrmidon are a caste of destruction savants and the Collegia Titanica set the ground trembling with the strides of their God-Engines.

THE RED PLANET

Greatest among the forge worlds of the Adeptus Mechanicus is Mars, the Red Planet. Situated in the Sol System, it is the birthplace of the Cult Mechanicus and the seat of its highest power. Mars is the fulcrum upon which the religious, political and military might of the Tech-Priests turns, its importance to the Imperium second only to its sister world, Holy Terra.

Mars is the original forge world. It is a planet given over in ages past to holy industry on an unprecedented scale. Ancient holo-reliquaries paint a picture of an isolated and terrifying era. Long before the Imperium, civil wars and unnamed disasters left Mars an irradiated wasteland, its frigid and toxic atmosphere unbreathable. A surviving culture underground relied heavily upon their remaining technology, so much so that its use and maintenance became ritualised. Technology became synonymous with life, their Machine God with Human survival.

On Mars' surface, rust red deserts of ferrous particulates blow along the fringes of vast accretions of soot- and chem-stained metropolises that encompass entire tectonic plates. Crackling capacitor banks the size of cities churn the thick and spoiled atmosphere, creating localised storms so persistent they are named as fixtures on ancient cartographic scrolls. Pollutants billow from mile-high stacks emblazoned with technoglyphs and crenelated with emitters that blare binharic canticles in praise of the Machine God. The ceaseless din of divine creation reverberates through the ground while plumes of cinders and sparks gush from huge, volcano-like vents. This is the perfection wrought by the Adeptus Mechanicus, and Mars' pre-eminence has seen its likeness remade in praiseworthy imitation time and again across the galaxy.

Tech-Priests throughout the Imperium are referred to collectively as the Priesthood of Mars, such is the planet's central role in their religion and internal politics. It is considered the holiest place of pilgrimage for adepts of the Cult Mechanicus, who are moved to rapture by the solar collector fields of Arcadia, their optics clicking furiously at the spiralled glory of Tantalus Hive and the rearing majesty of Olympus Mons, wherein resides the Fabricator General of Mars. As political and religious ruler of the Red Planet, the Fabricator General is ex officio head of the Adeptus Mechanicus, and holds a permanent position as one of the High Lords of Terra.

All forge worlds owe nominal fealty to Mars, and its ruler is vested with a divine right over all others, judging on matters of doctrine and legitimising contentious articles of trade. Few, however, slavishly submit to the Red Planet's superiority. Discoveries of ancient techno-arcana are often hidden rather than revealed to Martian eyes, schisms in theology and competition for resources can mar relationships for centuries and on occasion small wars have even broken out. Neither is Mars itself a homogenous, unitary domain; sub-sects conduct treasonous research or plot for power, hacking rival power wells, annexing territory or appropriating assets. Most forge worlds, though, solemnly respect the Red Planet's historical primacy. Many include elements of its ruddy livery in their own attire as a tacit recognition of this power – whether genuinely felt or not – and Mars is viewed as speaking with the authority of the Machine God. Thus, its Fabricator General is well versed in complex and aggressive factionalised interests, making their position on the council of High Lords relatively secure against assassination, coercion and deception.

AN ANCIENT ORDER

The Cult Mechanicus predates the unification of Terra in the 30th Millennium, though by how long remains a matter of fierce debate. It is tentatively accepted that the surviving remnants of technologically adept diaspora solidified their faith – and their hold over Mars – as the darkness of the Age of Strife receded. The horrors of that era, when so much data was destroyed and so many technologies lost to Mankind, haunt the Adeptus Mechanicus to this day. Oblique references to lost works in the most ancient of Mars' data-stacks hint at the despatch of missions to Terra and beyond. From the cradle of Humanity, the Tech-Priests took what they needed; shards of archeotech and slivers of archived data from Mankind's lost past, while techno-barbarian tribes warred over its surface.

By the time the Emperor quashed his rivals and bound Terra under his leadership, Mars was fully indoctrinated as a theocratic civilisation that worshipped the Machine God. The Emperor's first step to reclaim the galaxy with his Great Crusade was to forge an alliance with the Tech-Priests, and with it the Mechanicum was born. In exchange for their unalloyed aid in providing weapons and wargear for his armies, and ships in which to carry them to the stars, the Emperor promised the Mechanicum access to the ancient data and esoteric machineries discovered on the worlds he would conquer.

Fully integrated into the burgeoning Imperium, the Mechanicum was not spared the galaxy-shattering civil war known to later millennia as the Horus Heresy. Tech-Priests serving aboard the traitors' warships, and whole forge worlds in thrall to the power and promises of Horus, supplied secret data and arms, pledging entire legions of Titans to the Arch-Traitor's cause. Mars itself was rocked by open warfare as Horus' agents sought to suborn the entire institution from within. Little of hard fact survives from this time, but in the period of rebuilding after the Heresy, forged anew and rededicated as the Adeptus Mechanicus, the Priesthood of Mars set to the expurgation and extermination of its traitor elements with a fanaticism born of the truly devout.

THE RING OF IRON

Surrounding Mars and incorporating the moon of Phobos is a circlet of interlinked dockyards, orbital transfer hubs, atmospheric scrubbers and toxic refineries too dangerous even to allow on the Red Planet's abused surface. Comprising many other installations including survey outposts and formidable defence platforms, this Ring of Iron is most notable for the huge warships and other large starfaring constructs that are built along its length in gigantic suspended docks.

KEEPERS OF DIVINE LORE

The ruling caste of the Adeptus Mechanicus are the Tech-Priests. They direct the mammoth endeavours of fabrication upon which the Imperium depends and lead the followers of the Machine God in unforgiving crusades of ruthless acquisition. The Tech-Priests hoard Mankind's legacy of knowledge, seeking an ever-closer union with their deity.

Within the continuum of the Human species – its extremities warped by genetic aberration and psychic renaissance – few appear as divorced from the common stock of Mankind as the Tech-Priests of the Cult Mechanicus. As acts of worship, they routinely replace what they see as fallible flesh with bizarre mechanical augmentation, seeing it as a way to move closer to the Machine God, and toward perfection. Bionic limbs, artificial appendages and cybernetic organs in great profusion and variety render the majority as biomechanical horrors, barely recognisable as Human. Some Tech-Priests sport skittering, multi-jointed legs or crawling track units as more efficient locomotion, while gilded armatures glistening with blessed dispersal fluids replace or supplement their arms. Their methods of communication can seem as inhuman

as their appearance. Tech-Priests speak a number of strange dialects that blend the machine tongue with those of the wider Human race. These include binharic cant, Lingua Technis, hexamathic code, noospheric bleed and Novabyte. Few outside the Tech-Priests' orders can comprehend them, and then only with specialist augmentation. To Human ears they are a squall of mechanical blurts, hisses and crackles, but they also transmit on frequencies well beyond biological detection. These languages are replete with internal self-references and fragments of ancient tongues once spoken by the Machine God's chosen in Mankind's ancient past.

Tech-Priests find little use for ambiguous, emotional interactions. Thus, many do not hesitate to embrace multi-lensed optics, rebreather arrays, olfactory

modules and cranial implants that end up obscuring or replacing their face. Some even dispense with their head entirely, their organic brain instead supported in crystal jars linked by complex neural interfaces.

Just as Tech-Priests' forms are complex and varied, so too is their meritocratic organisation and hierarchy. Throughout the Imperium, individuals undertaking roles as Enginseers, Lexmechanics, Technoshamans and Noospheric Spectocrats can be seen upon many worlds and ships, accompanying Mankind's armies and tending to their engines of war. The Tech-Priests' ranks become more esoteric and inscrutable deeper inside the Adeptus Mechanicus' theocratic layers. Each forge world is led by a Fabricator General, the most technically adept and knowledgeable

HOLY ORDERS

MAGI
PRIME HERMETICON
LORD DOGMA
MECHAE MORIBUNDUS
INVICTUS ACQUISITOR
GERONTOCRAT
DATA-PREDATOR

GENETORS
MAGOS BIOLOGIS
ARCH-CHYMIST
GRAND PARASITE
METASURGEON
CORPUS ILLUMINATOR
GENETOR EXTREMIS

LOGI
LEXICO ARCANUS
BIBLIOPHILIAC
HYPER-RATIONALIST
MONITOR MALEVOLUS
INFO-EXECUTIONER
BIOCOGITATUS

ARTISANS
FORGE LORD
MECHASAPIENT
PRAETOR ELECTROID
CYBERSMITH
TECHNOARCHEOLOGIST
NECROMECHANIC

among their kind. Under this august individual is the world's Fabricator Locum, the masters of the forge temples, overseers of bionically-augmented thralls and a dizzying array of others that can be called upon for their unique knowledge. The term 'Tech-Priest' covers many thousands of roles, specialities and titles that are bestowed or adopted in a shifting matrix of power, some unique to their forge world or espoused only within a single sub-cult. Genetors probe the mysteries of the biological, creating strange cybernetic creature-amalgams and slaughtering xenos beyond number to uncover their alien frailties. Artisans create wondrous devices of archaic beauty and deadly effect, their ornate weapons and filigreed wargear highly coveted throughout the Imperium. Magi of countless kinds plumb the depths of increasingly narrow ravines of arcane know-how, heedless of the cost in their thrall-servants' lives, while Logi dig with acquisitive intensity through the physical and abstract strata of the universe, with pure information as their goal.

While those Tech-Priests in service to senior magisters are bound to their

master's obsessions and intrigues, more powerful adepts have few limitations on the avenues of holy knowledge they pursue. Tech-Priests Manipulus shape and wield the Motive Force – that aspect of the Machine God that grants vitality to all things, mechanical and biological. Others focus on the disciplines of metallurgy, alchemical synthesis, psychic resonance, gravitic theodominance and countless more that all contribute to the grinding Imperial war machine.

Tech-Priests do not shy away from the horrors of war. The demonstration of the Machine God's primacy in the universe and the application of their destructive,

theological devices are an opportunity to be grasped with fervour. Many replace more delicate mechanical appendages with war forms, steel shod bionics fitted with esoteric weaponry. The most senior adepts, in charge of calculating grand strategies and directing the zealous forces under their command, will adopt the title of Dominus. They will bend their considerable mental prowess and all the computational and logistical resources at their behest to the complete annihilation of the foe. Though the title is commonly temporary, some Tech-Priests choose to remain a Dominus, addicted to the superiority and divine power such a position grants.

The intricate web of shifting religious, political, technological and philosophical leanings within the Adeptus Mechanicus is bewildering to those outside the priesthood. Yet even as sub-cults, movements and schisms are in constant flux, certain Holy Orders are commonly recognised on the majority of forge worlds. Tech-Priests who subscribe to their broad tenets, while experts in sometimes wildly divergent matters of Cult doctrine, will strive to apply their knowledge in an established form. With the great power and autonomy that especially resourceful Tech-Priests can accumulate, some even invent tyrannical honorifics for themselves.

SKITARII LEGIONS

On limbs of hardened alloy march the cohorts of the Skitarii. They are soldiers of the Machine God and form the armies that answer to the Tech-Priests of the Cult Mechanicus. They glory in their augmented forms, granted the knowledge by their masters that each calculated kill and every grinding victory is achieved under the unblinking gaze of their deity.

The Skitarii are warriors made. Many were once part of the numberless pools of forcibly indentured labourers, or else vat-grown in mass flesh farms. No matter their origin, those who serve their forge world as Skitarii are zealously loyal and fanatically devoted to the Cult Mechanicus. Their masters refashion their bodies, replacing fallible ligaments and flesh with titanium servomotors and bionic musculature. The Skitarii see the Tech-Priests as prophets and intermediaries, each binharic order issued from on high as a holy commandment calibrated to stimulate awe and reverence.

Units of Skitarii operate under the leadership of their primary warrior, typically an Alpha or Princeps. Together, these units comprise a maniple, an organisational unit within the forge

world's military. Maniples are constituent parts of cohorts that in turn are part of macroclades. Maniples are assigned an identifying sigil drawn from the archaic and inscrutable symbology to which the Adeptus Mechanicus is heir. Through an interlocking system of cohorts and the even larger macroclades, each maniple, unit and individual Skitarius understands their place within the hierarchy of their forge world's military might.

While command at the higher levels is orchestrated with mechanical precision by individual Tech-Priests, Skitarii are not mindless automatons. Experienced Skitarii Marshals conduct independent operations along parameters defined by their masters. They utilise inloaded tactical schematics, meticulous planning and intuitive leaps of logic to respond to local divergences of kill

ratios and geospatial positioning. Rapid reassessment of enemy capabilities enable individual units to outwit those who believe they have the better of the Machine God's faithful. The information acquired is broadcast back along the nodes of command, informing hundreds of decisions per second, and is implemented to crush the enemy. When facing a lost cause, and even unto death, Skitarii continue to transmit stacks of data back to the Tech-Priests, harvested by multi-spectrum analysers, auto-filter optics, vox synthesisers and echolalic reverberators. The adepts of the Machine God care not if a hundred, a thousand or a million of their fanatical warriors fall in battle. The Skitarii are tools to be employed in the destruction of Mankind's enemies, a worthy sacrifice to absolute dominion. The data acquired by these fallen soldiers provides yet more

ARTISANAL APPARATUSES

The weapons employed by the Skitarii Legions are as ancient in form as they are advanced in technology. Galvanic rifles are said to be modelled on the hunting flintlocks of Mars' past. In the hands of the relentless Rangers who bear them, they are precision tools whose servitor-bullets burn out their target's potential energy on contact. Arc weapons employ permacapacitors and unleash blinding bolts of the Motive Force, while the depleted transuranium shell of an arquebus can puncture a tank as easily as an enemy leader's skull.

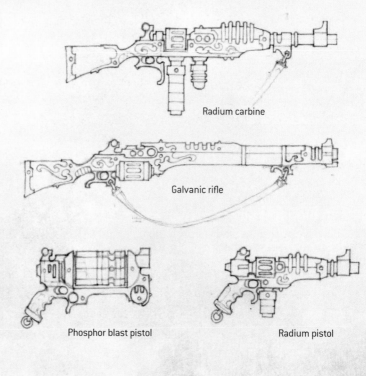

Radium carbine

Galvanic rifle

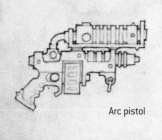

Arc pistol

Phosphor blast pistol

Radium pistol

knowledge of the foes' weaknesses, and feeds the grim computation of Adeptus Mechanicus strategy.

As carefully crafted weapons, a forge world's Skitarii fulfil as broad or as specialised a role as the Tech-Priests require of them, bearing the arcane technologies of their religious orders to war. Rad-saturated Vanguard are front-line troopers who weaponise the debilitating aura that infuses them, advancing relentlessly and rendering the battlefield as inimical to life as the Grystpits on Mars with volleys of irradiated carbine fire. Those promoted from the infantry maniples may be allocated to the Serberys corps, long range outriders or aggressive line breakers mag-locked atop loping, mechanical cybercanids.

Many Skitarii are re-fashioned into more particular forms, either as necessity or dogmatic tradition dictates. The Sicarians are warrior-clades comprised of hyper-aggressive and sinister combatants. Some, codified as Ruststalkers, hunt as gladiatorial assassins, their transonic blades and claws fused permanently into their bionic appendages, while Infiltrators pick their way stealthily across the most abused of landscapes, emitting multi-sensory 'white noise' to confuse and disable their prey. Perhaps strangest of all are the Pteraxii, routinely implanted with limb-stumps that plug into hyper-reactive, membranous wing packs or the control systems of aerial gunships. They undertake purgation missions in orbital docks and the dark, girded rafters of manufactorums, but hungrily turn their weapons upon more dangerous prey at their masters' command.

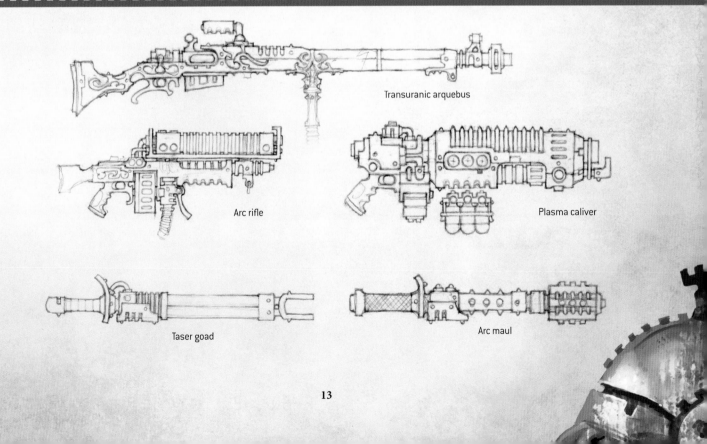

Transuranic arquebus

Arc rifle

Plasma caliver

Taser goad

Arc maul

WAR ZONE:
METALICA

The forces of Chaos, led by the Death Guard, poured their filth into the Charadon Sector, centred on the Metalica System. Forge world Metalica launched counter-offensives in scores of systems, calculating its own borders to be secure. Yet the traitors' power was not so easily held at bay. When the Metalica System was attacked, its quarry world of Plenitas saw fierce fighting.

Labour revolts and agitation among Metalica's millions-strong indentured workforce, particularly on the quarry world of Plenitas, had been rising as the forge world's Fabricator General had dispersed the system's resources to defend the wider sub-sector. Nevertheless, Plenitas' Skitarii garrison had been bolstered to enforce the maintenance of production quotas among the serf clans. Quantities of rare metals, magnesic ores and ferrumite once more flowed, yet it was a temporary reprieve.

After some months, Metalica high command suddenly received disturbing reports from more than a dozen mining operations on Plenitas. In mere days, heretical cults had revealed themselves, servitor units had malfunctioned and some form of transmechanical corruption had spread to some of the mammoth mining engines that now altered course and headed for subterranean forge complexes. Metalica rushed entire cohorts of Skitarii to the site, alongside macro-transports laden with giant, destructive engines of the Centurio Ordinatus. After three days, rampant electro-viruses and madness had bloomed across Plenitas' surface, from the central hub of Crater Valley to the astropathic relay at Hypea Mons. These maladies advanced in quickening waves until, at their height, they coincided with the opening of a warp rift in the heart of the Metalica system. In the dark days that followed, Mankind came to know this rift as the Sore, and from it poured an even greater threat.

Rather than dash themselves against Metalica's rigid system defences, the Death Guard had employed the rotting death throes of an entire world in a distant system to eat into the flesh of space and time. Like a maggot burrowing through a corpse, their sorcery had chewed open the rift, allowing immense and ancient warships to traverse the passage and lumber forth from the Sore. From them came attack craft bearing Heretic Astartes, Daemon Engines and all manner of other corrupted horrors.

FERMATON PRIMUS

REPATRIARCHUS MECHANICUM: -874.41X

The Overseer-Imperator of Plenitas, Teagh Chi-Vonn, had adopted her Dominus war protocols as soon as empyric energies of the Sore had been detected. Connected to the world's macro-cogitator banks, Chi-Vonn personally managed the overall strategy. The quarry world was a source of incredible wealth for Metalica, but of far greater value were the technologies employed upon Plenitas. The world's resources were scattered through hyperdense minerals, requiring unique mechanisms and refinery processes to extract. Mining engines thought to date back to the system's colonisation were relics beyond any price, as were the two atomic smelters, – Janussan and Denmar-Vb – and fleets of servo-operated geodelvers.

Dominus Chi-Vonn, in noospheric communion with her senior Magi, formulated a strategy of tri-fermaton. This three-phase operation would brutally purge the corrupted elements already on Plenitas and hold back the worst the Death Guard threw at them, all while preparing for the retrieval and repatriation of the most sacred technologies and engine cores. At Gheren Hive, an uprising of rabid plague cultists was corralled by Pteraxii Sterylizors and squadrons of Serberys Sulphurhounds. Together they encircled huge mobs of the infected, driving back hundreds of sore-ridden heretics and techno-possessed servitors into flame-lit service tunnels before sealing them inside. Meanwhile, the attempted sabotage of a promethium repository by cultists in the dockyards of Thryssen Refinery, was uncovered by Sicarian Infiltrators of Delta Maniple. The reinforcing cohort of Vanguards and Rangers intercepted the cultists' own rearguard and destroyed the insurrectionist's control centre.

FERMATON SECUNDUS

REPATRIARCHUS MECHANICUM: -307.01B

The Death Guard of Lord Fecuthrott the Reaper made planetfall at seven strategically important sites, including the relay at Hypea Mons and the magnesic processing facility of Kharonar. At Crater Valley, Lord Fecuthrott launched a mass offensive. The valley's network of artificial geothermal vents not only fed the world's power networks, but was the site of the planet's mercantile space port and a hub of ore refining. Fecuthrott flooded the valley floor with hordes of Poxwalkers, mutated Chaos Spawn and rabid cultists, driving them forward in a vast wedge. Chi-Vonn's junior Magi at Crater Valley also reported the thermal signatures of dozens of armoured vehicles and impure power armour, but clouds of dust and black insects made visual confirmation impossible.

Screaming waves of plague-marked cultists ran forward in waves, sent in to die and deplete the ammunition of the massed Metalican defences. Their electoos of former servitude served as unintended target marks, and dozens fell every second. Bombing runs by Archaeopter Fusilaves and darting forays by kill teams of Sicarian Ruststalkers disrupted the shambling attackers' forward ranks. Chi-Vonn estimated it would not stop the advance, but she had enumerated the frequency and angle of attacks to slow it down. It gave her Magi time to deconsecrate the magnastatic seals at the valley's head and release the planet's fiery wrath. From the bowels of a magma chamber, kept in check for millennia, gushed a blazing river of lava and clouds of searing gases. Thousands of the Death Guard's rotten vanguard were immolated. The resultant morass of melted corpses and cooling lava forced the Death Guard's armoured convoy and elite infantry into a circuitous redeployment that bought Chi-Vonn a few more precious hours.

The Dominus continued to feed yet more cohorts of devoted Skitarii into the meat grinders that pockmarked Plenitas. The evacuation of the irreplaceable and most sacred engines began in earnest, but it was a slow process. The vaunted artefact-engines of the Ordinatus released their final incandescent payloads or kept firing their unique energy weapons until the last possible moment before these singular leviathans too were marked for retrieval. Hastily requested lifter barges, fortified against atmospheric descent, had arrived from Metalica, and into their cavernous holds were raised devices of exquisite and ancient design. The careful procedures of supplication and decontamination were carried out as swiftly as was dared, the Tech-Priests fearful of angering the machine spirits of those being evacuated. Super-heavy capacitor ships grazed the atmosphere above the holy sites, ionizing the air for miles around and sanctifying the ground with coruscating sparks of power.

Chi-Vonn surprised her junior Tech-Priests by delegating oversight of these operations to them. She redoubled her efforts to curtail the Death Guard's victories, absorbing ever more sources of data as she orchestrated the global defence. She monitored teleportation flares, redirecting reinforcements to their location within nanoseconds, and abandoned battles she saw as inconsequential.

The evacuation of Plenitas' prized assets was mostly successful, though there were tragic losses. At Moribundus Temple, the atomic smelter Denmar-Vb was destroyed when a rogue mining engine broke into the underforge from below. Far less tragic losses included the surviving cohorts of Skitarii and the remaining loyal clans of labour serfs. They were commanded to maintain their battle protocols unto victory or termination, as the lifter barges bore their precious cargoes back to Metalica itself.

THE ARCANE AND THE ANCIENT

The Tech-Priests' strange rites, biomechanical servants and ability to work incomprehensible devices make them figures of awe and fear throughout most of the Imperium. Strange creations lumber forward at their command, energies that primitives consider magical are summoned and technologies from ages best forgotten are unleashed in destructive tempests.

The Adeptus Mechanicus draw upon millennia of surviving human technology and the mysteries of their own arcane religion to create not only slab-sided battle tanks, huge capacitors and city-sized vessels, but far stranger and more sinister creations. Servo skulls crafted from the craniums of loyal Imperial subjects hover on anti-grav thrusters. Gene-cloned familiars packed with advanced sensory suites perch in the shadows while entirely mechanical cyber-constructs growl through vox grilles at their side. In their creation, Tech-Priests employ scarce metals, carboniferous fibroids, bone, infraglass, seventh phase helionite and rarer substances in their efforts to duplicate the construction formulae set down by their predecessors. Many creations are known only within the closed orders of the Cult Mechanicus, while some are granted as gifts to staunch allies. By far the most common creations are servitors.

SERVITORS

The servitor complement of even a single forge world will typically number in the tens, or even hundreds, of millions. Many were once criminals accused of any one of the Imperium's byzantine and ruthlessly enforced laws – from low-born black marketeers, to outmanoeuvred members of the political elite, or Inquisitorial enforcers who saw too much. Forcibly given a second chance to serve the Imperium as a useful servant, such men and women are now grim husks of their former selves. Each individual is mind-wiped, chemically and surgically lobotomised so that their memories and personality are a blank slate – in theory at least, for there are tales of servitors retaining vestiges of consciousness. The condemned is then augmented to fulfil any number of countless roles in manufactorums, dockyards, refineries and anywhere else that requires menial and repetitive labour. Most have one or both arms cut away and replaced with bionic armatures fitted with grappling claws, laser scalpels, servo manipulators, heavy lifting rigs or even weapons.

In the case of battle servitors, such as those of the Kataphron class, many specimens are bisected at the hips and fitted with industrial track units capable of grinding over the harshest of terrain. Kataphron Breachers are among the largest and most potent of these living weapons, each augmented with additional, vat-grown flesh grafts. They are heavily armoured, designed to break apart enemy battle lines and fortifications while ignoring the small arms fire of defenders. Once their proximity clarions chime, they return fire with bolts of holy energy and wrenching gaol-fields from heavy arc rifles or torsion cannons before crushing the remaining foes with their piston-driven claws. In contrast, Kataphron Destroyers bear few close combat attachments, and are instead equipped with additional devastating firepower. As mobile weapons platforms, they mount giant cannons of ancient design that can crush or incinerate their masters' foes, alongside secondary weapons that spit roaring gouts of flame or streams of incandescent phosphor. Tech-Priests often surround themselves with whole clades of Kataphron battle servitors, and endless numbers of them are created day and night on every forge world. They are all ultimately tools to be expended by the Adeptus Mechanicus with no more thought than a soldier would empty a gun clip. After battle,

ONAGER DUNECRAWLERS

The Onager Dunecrawler is a walker-engine akin to a multi-legged battle tank. It easily negotiates dangerous battlefields as it brings its arsenal to bear, its hull bristling with heavy weaponry of archaic design. Dunecrawlers can blast apart squadrons of aircraft, punch holes in traitor battle engines or atomise enemy commanders in beams of blue light. The engine owes its origins to the Mars Universal Land Engine, fashioned by the famed technoarcheologist Arkhan Land. Intended as a workhorse that could escort its masters across the inhospitable wastes of Mars in relative safety, the machine proved so successful it was inevitably repurposed as a weapon of war – though only after many centuries of careful religious discussion and rigorous scriptural interpretation.

To its enmeshed crew and the Skitarii formations alongside which it often fights, the Dunecrawler is no mere weapon, but a walking reliquary of sacred technologies protected by the hand of the Machine God. Overlapping Emanatus force shielding fields disperse hostile energies into the atmosphere, and incoming projectiles are transmuted into little more than flashes of light and tangs of ozone.

damaged units are recovered for re-use, the powerful weapons and sturdy chassis re-sanctified. Any remnants of the Human at their core are unceremoniously dumped before being replaced by another hapless auto-volunteer from amongst the Tech-Priests' seemingly endless supply.

IRONSTRIDER ENGINES

Servitors are also permanently integrated into many of the Adeptus Mechanicus' more complex devices. The motive engines ridden to war by the corps of Sydonian Dragoons and Ironstrider Ballistarii are each fitted with a mono-task servitor that serves as a steering conduit. The Ironstrider engine they form a part of is a stilt-limbed combat walker perfected by the Tech-Priest Aldebrac Vingh in early M33. The limbless and sightless servitor exists as an interface between the commands issued by the experienced Skitarii warrior mounted on top and the near-perfect perpetual motion dynamo at the engine's core.

Sydonian Dragoons operate as swift-moving shock troops, wreathed in clouds of ochre incense as they mount deadly charges with their pronged taser lances. Their ranks often comprise the most zealous of a forge world's Skitarii, and are viewed by others of their cohort as chivalric hunters, marking their quarry with radiating shot so they can track them down no matter where they run. The Ironstrider Ballistarii are also constantly on the move, stalking the fringes of their maniple to find ideal firing positions and then moving again before the enemy can retaliate. Their pilots are marksmen beyond compare, often drawn from the ranks of veteran Ranger units. Steadied by gyroscopic stabilisers, Ironstrider Ballistarii form stable firing platforms for their powerful cognis heavy weapons with which they hunt enemy vehicles and commanders.

ELECTRO-PRIESTS

Congregations of Electro-Priests embody many of the arcane and fanatical aspects of the Cult Mechanicus. All are devoted to the Motive Force, the aspect of the Machine God that adepts of the Adeptus Mechanicus preach is the spark that drives all systems, biological and mechanical. It is the fire that leaps from

neuron to neuron and the illumination that reignites cold reactor cores. The Motive Force runs like a current through the bodies of Electro-Priests, channelled by electoos and amplified by their fervour so that their bodies crackle with power. Implanted under the skin of Electro-Priests, electoos connect their entire nervous system, sending bio-electric pulses potent enough to incinerate incoming projectiles. An example of the less obvious, but no less bizarre technologies to emerge from the forge temples of the Adeptus Mechanicus, electoos can be made to be nearly invisible. Alternatively, they can be made to radiate vibrantly through the flesh of those who bear them, serving as proud brands bestowed by the Machine God. These subcutaneous circuitries range from small metallic wafers, to silvery streams of motile nano-servitors and even full body networks. Simple versions are worn by every one of the Machine God's worshippers and can be remotely accessed to provide a wealth of identifying and hierarchical data. Few rival the extent and complexity of those borne by the Electro-Priest brotherhoods.

How this holy resource is employed is at the heart of an antagonistic schism among the Electro-Priests. Those of the Corpuscarii faction believe in spreading the light of the Machine God's bounty. They advance while chanting binharic litanies, building up the energy within their bodies and discharging it in gouts of power from their electrostatic gauntlets. These electrocuting bolts grant unbelievers one ecstatic moment of enlightenment before burning them from the inside out. Their rivals among the Fulgurite brotherhoods see such discharges of electrical power as wasting the Machine God's finite favour. They consider it a vile sin, and it is one they see also in their deity's enemies, whose very existence fritters away the holy Motive Force. Rather than slaying from afar, Fulgurites smite their enemies face to face with long-hafted electroleech staves. These draw the energy from those they strike and store it in capacitor cells on the Electro-Priest's back. In the wake of the Fulgurites, enemy vehicles are left cold and dead, while once-living creatures lie motionless, their nervous system and organs stilled forever.

LEGIO CYBERNETICA

When the automatons of the Legio Cybernetica go to war, the ground shakes with the thunderous stamping of their robotic feet. The air is filled with praise-blurts glorifying the Omnissiah emitted from rasping voxes, and psalm-programmes grind loud over the din of war. They are the Ever-Faithful, each an ancient servant of the Machine God.

KASTELAN ROBOTS

Kastelan Robots are possessed of immense physical might and rugged stamina, and harbour no sense of doubt or weakness. Each is an unliving giant, assigned a specific war-purpose by its Datasmith master. These mighty constructs have fought the Imperium's foes since the founding of the Mechanicum, and many forge worlds claim to have examples that have served them for millennia before this. This is within the realms of possibility, for the technology used to produce such powerful constructs predates the Imperium of Man. Yet the secrets of their creation are now all but lost, and so the resanctified portions used to maintain those that survive mean a great many bear elements that are surely well over ten thousand years old.

The bulk of Kastelan Robots alone allows them to weather enormous storms of heavy fire with impunity, but they are also equipped with devices that emit invisible, thrumming repulsor grids using technology from a bygone age. The surrounding cages of force cause most incoming fire to fizzle out against the unseen barrier, but should attacks strike the grid at the right angle,

they will deflect back at the firer as if cast back by the vengeful hand of the Omnissiah himself.

Kastelan Robots fight in maniples – self-contained units that are sub-divisions of the legion – composed of between two and six automata. In battle they follow carefully programmed battle protocols, though they can only follow one at any given time. Should the protocol need to change, a specialist Tech-Priest such as a Cybernetica Datasmith can adjust the program even during the fury of intense firefights. Should no one change the protocol a Kastelan Robot is following, it will follow that protocol ad infinitum until its power reserves are exhausted – which might take weeks of relentless fighting – or until it is destroyed. It is not unheard of for a maniple of Kastelan robots to stride into a lake of highly corrosive industrial run-off or go about reducing a city to ruins even when the last foe has been purged from it, all because it is following protocols no longer applicable to the situation.

Some maniples of Kastelan Robots appear to have spent millennia following strange directions and protocols programmed into them by masters thousands of

years dead. These ancient machines call no forge world home, and are instead itinerant. They often arrive in battle, unheeded, their appearance taken as a sign of the Machine God's favour. Constructs such as 13-Tor, known as the Automongrel of the Grainan Stellar Drawbridge, and Dostoyon Vladimus 12, the Iron Ghost of Farewell Secundus, fight until battle is won, seemingly receptive to directives from Tech-Priests. Afterwards, they disappear again, not seen perhaps for centuries.

There are a number of battle protocols that a maniple can be programmed to follow, such as that of the Conqueror. When this is activated, the Kastelan Robots advance towards the foe, their stride turning to a loping run. They close upon the enemy with remarkable speed and become battering rams. Their barrel-sized fists swing like wrecking balls, pulverising flesh, crushing armour and punching through ferrocrete with equal ease. When the Protector protocol is activated, the Kastelans become bastions of firepower, turning their heavy weaponry upon the foe, re-routing blessed subroutines from rapid locomotion to precision bombardment. These automata can also be equipped

THE MIND IN THE MACHINE

The Legio Cybernetica's origins lie with the tech-savants who first experimented with artificial life in the Dark Age of Technology. These highly curious individuals built great hosts of automata and gave them the power of independent thought. This was a terrible mistake, one that led to awful consequences for the whole of Humanity. From that point on the use of the dreaded silica animus was outlawed forever. Those who dared attempt to resurrect this technology were tortured until death, but this did not stop others from attempting to utilise the technology to make thinking machines, believing they could avoid the mistakes of Mankind's past. Some attempted to design constructs

with the minds of loyal beasts. Others went a darker route, blending their machines with essences from the empyrean. All these attempts led to disastrous consequences. Fragmented accounts and rotting datastacks suggest that Warmaster Horus cared not for the potential damage these engines could cause, sponsoring their insane creators and winning them over to his side. These depraved individuals became a part of the Dark Mechanicum, an intentionally indefinite moniker for those hereteks spoken of only by the Priesthood of Mars, and even then in whispered code. Yet the fear and dark legend of armies of thinking-machines persists throughout the Imperium.

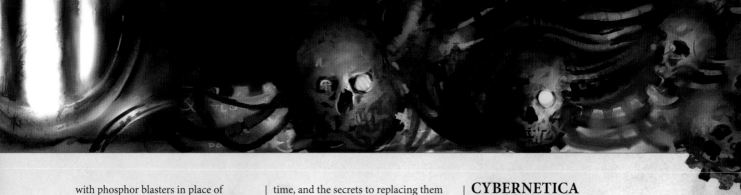

with phosphor blasters in place of powered fists, perfect for those Tech-Priests who require enormous firepower. When armed in this way, and once the applicable ballistics subroutines have been triggered, the robots pour a storm of incandescent, glowing shot into the enemy. The burning white spheres cling tenaciously to their targets, sizzling wildly as they burrow through armour and melt into flesh.

In millennia past, the robots of the Legio Cybernetica numbered enough to lay waste to entire alien empires – but these days are thought to be no more. Many of the hallowed machines have been lost to time, and the secrets to replacing them have been all but forgotten. Because of this, it takes a Tech-Priest of surpassing rank to authorise their use in battle, and forge worlds will sanction extreme expense to recover those Kastelans that have fallen in battle – from sending in waves of Skitarii to cover the extraction of their fragments to funding an Explorator Crusade to quest after rumours of an intact specimen. Yet these machines continue to fight on the front lines of the most crucial wars. To the Tech-Priests who consider the flesh to be weak, commanding these constructs is like commanding the angels of the Omnissiah himself.

CYBERNETICA DATASMITHS

Cybernetica Datasmiths are a specialist rank of Tech-Priest that program the robots of the Legio Cybernetica at the maniple level, and are expected to do so even during the most furious fighting. They are thus equipped with a wide array of weapons and arcana from their forge world's arsenals. Their gamma pistol fire beams of ionizing radiation that can reduce a human to ash, burn holes through fortress walls or reduce the armour of battle tanks into a ferrous ooze. Many Datasmiths also bear prehensile dataspikes, which can steal the secrets of enemy machines within heartbeats of being stabbed into the engines' cortices. With this powerful wargear, Cybernetica Datasmiths can defend themselves and still continue their vital work of overseeing their robotic charges.

For ten thousand years, the robots of the Legio Cybernetica have obeyed their masters – save for those few units with irreversibly fixed protocols. They are not controlled by the bio-plastic cerebra and nerve-like tendril webs of Mechanicum constructs, but by sanctified doctrina wafers: fusions of biomatter and electronics often in even shorter supply than the robots themselves. No bigger than the cards of the Emperor's Tarot, these slivers of necromantic wetware are entrusted to those Cybernetica Datasmiths that accompany the robot maniples to war. These wafers are inserted into a dataslot hidden behind a robot's chestplate, and the wafer's command protocol dictates every action of its host's behaviour. Should a Datasmith wish to change the behaviour of their charges, they must manually exchange the wafer currently inserted into a robot's dataslot for another. It follows naturally that this poses a risk. If the Datasmith has been slain, or if a wafer or the dataslot becomes damaged, the robot's protocols may be irreversible. This limitation hampers the flexibility of robot maniples who may not be able to adapt to fluid battle plans. Both of these the Cult Mechanicus accepts. Hardwiring independent thought into battle automata is strictly forbidden by the Crimson Accords of Mars, laws older than the Imperium itself.

EXPLORATOR FLEETS

In their pursuit of knowledge and technology, the Tech-Priests and their legions of cyborg servants launch holy fleets to explore the frontiers of the Imperium. Though ostensibly religious processions of preservation and enquiry, these vast agglomerations of military might are possessed of the power to destroy whole armies before them.

The Quest for Knowledge is the consuming crusade of the Adeptus Mechanicus. They see it as procuring the data, resources and artefacts that are rightfully the Machine God's due. A forge world's Explorator fleets are the primary means by which this sacred duty is undertaken. Each is a unique armada of vessels despatched to deafening hails of binharic hymns. They must be prepared to wrest control of ancient technology from unenlightened heathens,

or to defend it against selfish or jealous usurpers, so each Fleet is packed with cohorts of armed Skitarii and countless devoted members of the priesthood, often with representatives of allied Knightly Houses and other Imperial forces. They set out to uncover lost fragments of Human technology, locate fresh resources or catalogue emergent xenos species and celestial phenomena. With the hopes, and the prestige, of their forge world riding with them, Explorator fleets delve

into unknown reaches of wilderness space, venturing to the fringes of the Astronomican's light. They are viewed as intrepid pioneers, accepting great risks for the greater glory of the Machine God.

Operating in isolation for decades, or even centuries, Explorator fleets must be self-sustaining, rapaciously plundering worlds of resources and forcibly requisitioning the contents of mercantile traders' holds. Rumours sometimes

EXPLORATOR FLEET PENTA-GAMMA 66Z3

The founding of Lucius' most ancient extant Explorator fleet – Penta-Gamma 66z3's – dates back to M34. Its original Explorator Majoris, Ehrlan Foss-Chrom, interpreted his holy commission of expanding Lucius' influence in the most efficient way he could perceive. The fleet traces a spherical route around the forge world, its progress expanding year by year, gradually bringing it to more distant systems. Foss-Chrom implanted unbreakable protocol imperatives into the command throne of the fleet's flagship, compelling every successor to rigidly follow his perfect strategy. Penta-Gamma 66z3 re-establishes contact with Lucius every few decades, and such momentous occasions are marked by the raising of honoured cohorts of Skitarii to reinforce the Fleet.

EXPLORATOR FLEET VENTRIS-SIGMATA 91

The Martian Explorator fleet Ventris-Sigmata 91 travels in an arcing parabola towards the unknown western rim. In addition to the military might of Mars, Ventris-Sigmata 91 bears a lance of Knights from House Krast. Like all Explorator fleets, it lost contact with its forge world when the Great Rift yawned wide. Through chance, or by the Omnissiah's will, the Fleet was thrust from the warp into a contested war zone. Ventris-Sigmata 91 aided the Iron Hands and Cyderic Combat Engineers they encountered in a hard-fought victory over a piratical flotilla of Aeldari. Even with contact re-established to Mars, the survivors of this gruesome conflict have since attached themselves to the fleet.

surface of them cannibalising vulnerable ships, sending in servitor details to cut them apart and press-ganging their crews into indentured servitude. Explorator fleets are overseen by a hardy and aggressive cabal of Tech-Priests with no doubt about the superiority of their endeavour. These Explorators comprise specialists in wildly divergent fields of expertise, theocratic logic and sacred interpretation. Having different philosophical approaches to the same specialism within a fleet often proves beneficial when cogitating rumours, sightings and hearsay from one system to another in search of arcana mechanicum – though more than one fleet has splintered along deep divides of opinion, their ships following different paths through the void towards perceived truth.

When an Explorator fleet reaches a world already subject to Imperial law, the Tech-Priests initiate a deep trawl of the planet's data networks. Vid-scalpers and info-miners are sunk into the deepest strata of the planet's datasphere; these predatory protocols rooting out any quirk of the world's technological base that hints at a more advanced past. Sump dwellers and frontier nomads are interrogated for myths of strange devices or lost settlements. Sometimes, even the whiff of ancient artifice suffices, and the Explorator fleet will deploy its strength. Such invasive tactics can lead to uneasy stand-offs with the world's native defence forces, though the unrest this incites has sometimes proven beneficial, as xenos- or Chaos-tainted subversives are stirred into revealing themselves.

Derelict worlds are scoured with deep penetrating auspex probes and continent-shaping earthmovers. Technoarcheologists sift through bedrock formations and beneath polar ice caps for telltale energy signatures or curiously regular density returns. Ancient battle sites are also prime targets for investigation. Fragments of STCs are among the most highly prized shards of archeotech, packed with condensed technical know-how from the days when the Machine God's chosen worked nigh-sorcerous miracles, or so it is said. While many Explorator fleets are given open-ended mandates, some are raised as Explorator crusades and tasked with the rediscovery of a specific legendary engine, lost forge temple or resource-rich planet.

EXPLORATOR CRUSADE GHEINT'S MONOPOLE

Named by Graia for the near mythical device it was launched to recover, Gheint's Monopole has accomplished incredible deeds in its long search. Yet while rumours have led them towards prized assets or corruptions to be smote, all have proved false trails for their true goal. The Explorator Crusade tracked an unusual emission only to discover unsanctioned hereteks tinkering with a planet's astropathic relay. Two sectors away upon an icy trojan planet, the Crusade's Technoarcheologists detected a semi-dormant Necron tomb, allowing their ships to obliterate the structure and xenos inside with orbital lance strikes. Three rich deposits of neo-promethium have been tapped and two forge temples newly consecrated – yet of the Monopole they seek, all they know is its name.

EXPLORATOR FLEET OMEGON-CRUCIATUS 54-9

The cataloguing of intelligent species among the stellar nurseries of the Trebint Cluster is the blinkered focus of the Stygies VIII Explorator fleet Omegon-Cruciatus 54-9. Conclaves of Tech-Priests orchestrate these investigations by partition their natural hatred for xenos in favour of data acquisition. Senior Magi Biologis, Genetors and Enginseers specialising in biological elucidation patiently take apart specimen after specimen to ensure no secret weakness eludes them. Omegon-Cruciatus 54-9 prepares prospective schedules of extermination for each new race they root out, taking aggressive action wherever they encounter more than the simplest alien technologies.

'BROADCAST THE PSALMS OF WAR TO
DRIVE THE MACROCLADES TO TRIUMPH.'

– EXCERPT FROM CANTICLES OF WAR
DOCTRINA ALPHA

MARS41

MARS

BIRTHPLACE OF THE CULT MECHANICUS

The Red Planet is the foundation stone of the Adeptus Mechanicus, and is vaunted as one of the holiest of all celestial orbs by its adherents, second only to Terra itself. Mars' arrogant Tech-Priests see themselves as the most blessed of the Machine God's followers, to which all others must pay an exacting measure of respect, and to whom is due a commensurate ratio of resources.

The zealotry of Mars' Tech-Priests is heralded by the constant buzz of static psalms, their obedient warriors incanting the holy rites to the Omnissiah as they march forward. Mars maintains its pre-eminence among the Adeptus Mechanicus by colonising worlds rich in resources, launching Explorator fleets to the fringes of the Imperium and raising monumental forge temples to the glory of the Machine God. Agents of Mars are spread throughout the galaxy, throughout Mankind's armed forces, among a great number of the Imperial Navy warships and are even found overseeing other forge worlds. The Red Planet counts among its empire more subservient industrialised worlds and forge moons than any of its peers, and great trails of machinery, ammunition and technological wonders flow between its holdings.

Mars' Tech-Priests are the heralds of the Machine God; they suffer no affront to the forge world's majesty and no suggestion that its creations are not the greatest. Their engines are blessed with the most holy unguents and their vast Skitarii cohorts exult in their role as the holy warriors of their deity's chosen realm. Though still considered mere tools by their Tech-Priest masters, the Martian Skitarii are inducted into selected lesser mysteries of the Cult Mechanicus, for if the Tech-Priests are the most blessed, then so must their tools and creations be. Marshals are implanted with stringent superiority protocols, making them unrelenting in their mobilisation of Mars' cohorts and fanatically driven to derive nothing less than perfection from those they direct.

In the mammoth logistical undertaking of the Indomitus Crusade, macroclades from the Red Planet accompany a great many of Guilliman's fleets. Fighting alongside contingents from across the Imperium, their warriors know they embody the martial honour of the Adeptus Mechanicus in the eyes of others, and will not be found wanting.

THE OMNISSIAH

The religion of the Adeptus Mechanicus is an aberration. The Ecclesiarchy promulgate that the Imperial Creed is Mankind's sole system of belief, and that any deviancy from it subject to a variety of inventive punishments. The worship of the Machine God, however, is allowed to continue and even spread without hindrance. This policy stems primarily from the fact that the Imperium could not exist without the Adeptus Mechanicus, and the prospective horrors of a cataclysmic civil war mean the Ecclesiarchy has no stated desire to force the Tech-Priests' conversion. The Ecclesiarchy's rationalisation of the Cult Mechanicus is also eased through the Tech-Priests' praise of the Omnissiah – a common aspect of the Machine God, with the terms sometimes synonymous. The Omnissiah is the Machine God made manifest, and the Priesthood of Mars believe the Emperor to be this manifestation. The Adeptus Mechanicus thus revere him not only as the Master of Mankind, but as an avatar of omniscience. It was to Mars that the Emperor came when his historic alliance was made with the Tech-Priests, and though no records are known to document this, the Omnissiah's blessing is something the Red Planet frequently reminds other forge worlds of. Despite this, there are sub-cults and factions who whisper that the Emperor is merely a prophet of the Machine God and not divine. Tensions quickly run high amid claims and counter-claims of tech-heresy and the ever-present shadow of potential schism.

The vaunted rank of Dominus is bestowed only on those of the Cult Mechanicus with a true talent for war; those who believe the supremacy of the Machine God is to be proven at every opportunity. It is a belief seldom held as fiercely as upon Mars itself.

FILE: OMEGA-7//832LB — ADEPTUS MECHANICUS

'THE OMNISSIAH KNOWS MY WORK, EVEN
IF OTHERS ARE TOO BLIND TO ACCEPT
AN OPUS OF GENIUS.'

— ARCHMAGOS DOMINUS CAWL

BELISARIUS CAWL

ARCHMAGOS DOMINUS, PRIME CONDUIT OF THE OMNISSIAH

Arcanologist and Fabricator, Tyrannus Mechanicum and Genetor Majoris, Belisarius Cawl augments and supersedes his numerous achievements as his demanding mind dictates. The shadow of Cawl's signature genius can be seen in many of the Imperium's greatest technologies of today, though their genesis dates back millennia.

Archmagos Dominus Belisarius Cawl was already old at the birth of the Imperium, over ten thousand years ago. During that span of ages the Tech-Priest has served Mars and the Machine God as a Forge Lord and a Lexico Arcanus, among other positions both known and unknown to his contemporaries. But it is in his role as Magos Biologis that Cawl's greatest mastery lies. It is rightfully said that the aged Archmagos Dominus has forgotten more knowledge – particularly about genetics – than all but the most studious adepts could ever hope to learn. Despite portions of his own memories having been stolen, and despite having twice suffered mindwiping, Cawl remains a tech-savant, a genius at the forefront of whatever field he trains his brilliant mind upon. Even amongst the ranks of the Adeptus Mechanicus, where artificial devices increase brain capacity and extend life beyond measure, such an accumulation of knowledge in multiple disciplines is exceedingly rare. The Priesthood of Mars ennoble such beings as Prime Conduits of the Omnissiah, or as a Dominatus Dominus – Master of Masters – and of those few still living who bear these titles, Cawl is by far the most active.

Belisarius Cawl dedicates himself to a multitude of projects, his mind leaping from the construction of Mars' largest macromag-cannon, to perfecting his stasis field work, or to the endless experiments he conducts within his city-sized laboratories housed in Mars' extensive underground complexes. The majority of these obsessive undertakings are done in secret. Cawl has so many projects running simultaneously that he has implemented multiple consciousnesses to track them, and has employed furtive measures to keep them hidden from rivals. Deep in sealed vaults, countless experiments await Cawl's multi-faceted servo-eyes.

Cawl's holdings on Mars belie his seeming independence from the political elite of the Red Planet. There are Forge Lords whose temples are aligned to receive the favour of the Fabricator General, and whose resources and power should far outstrip Cawl's. Yet his manufactorums are far more extensive than most. They thunder through the ember-lit nights and smog-shrouded days of Mars, churning out esoteric materiel and exquisitely crafted constructions. As Cawl's accelerated cogitation sprints from design to design, so does he reconfigure his plasma forges, magnacoil weavers, crystalloy aligners and other immense, sigil-carved engines so that their production keeps pace with his energetic deliberations. Quite from where the aged Dominus receives the entirety of his insights, patronage and resources isn't established to the satisfaction of some of his peers. Junior adepts whisper that Cawl's cubic miles' worth of interlaced workshop fortresses hum with the secrets muttered by millions of obedient machine spirits, and that his occasional lapses of memory signal the effort of constantly processing the binharic babel.

Since reloading a portion of his stored memories, the ancient Tech-Priest has become forgetful, prone to spending recuperative decades within his own stasis crypts. Yet such prolonged periods offline inspire Cawl to once more take to the field in his hunt for knowledge. It is during such times that Cawl dons the mantle of Archmagos Dominus, gathering about him Skitarii Legions and maniples of the Legio Cybernetica. Although Mars is his home world, other forge worlds often place troops beneath Cawl's command, asking only that he shares any knowledge accumulated.

On the battlefield Cawl is a force to be reckoned with, and he fearlessly scuttles into the thick of the fighting. Most enemy weapons fire is thwarted by Cawl's refractor field. Yet even when parts of his mechanised body are blasted off, cables snake out to effect immediate repairs and to swarm any foes that come close. The hunched figure is a whir of activity as cogitators adjust firing angles, broadcast orders to his troops and dispense the imperative word of the Machine God. Amidst the maelstrom of combat, the Tech-Priest himself remains calm, his mind assessing threats, predicting enemy attacks and calculating victory probabilities.

DEEDS THAT FILL DATA-STACKS

Belisarius Cawl has invented dozens of weapons, uncovered scores of STCs and quested for knowledge across the galaxy, even once venturing into the Eye of Terror. Malfunctions, erasures and jumbled transformats have left vast holes in Cawl's memories, but what remains fills vaulted halls the size of a battle cruiser. There, in binharic code stacks, are mountains of information – from the hundreds of xenos races that he helped drive to extinction, to the schematic details of wonder-engines lost since the Age of Technology; from the galactic census during the Great Crusade to studies of communication difficulties in the aftermath of the Great Rift. It is a knowledge-hoard unlike any other. So vast is this information stockpile that Cawl no longer remembers how he obtained huge portions of it. Still, that knowledge – along with the potent genetic material contained within the device known as the Sangprimus Portum – allowed Cawl to successfully complete the creation of the Primaris Space Marines and implement the Ultima Founding. Despite the import of this act to the Imperium, Belisarius Cawl holds that he has even greater experiments currently in development.

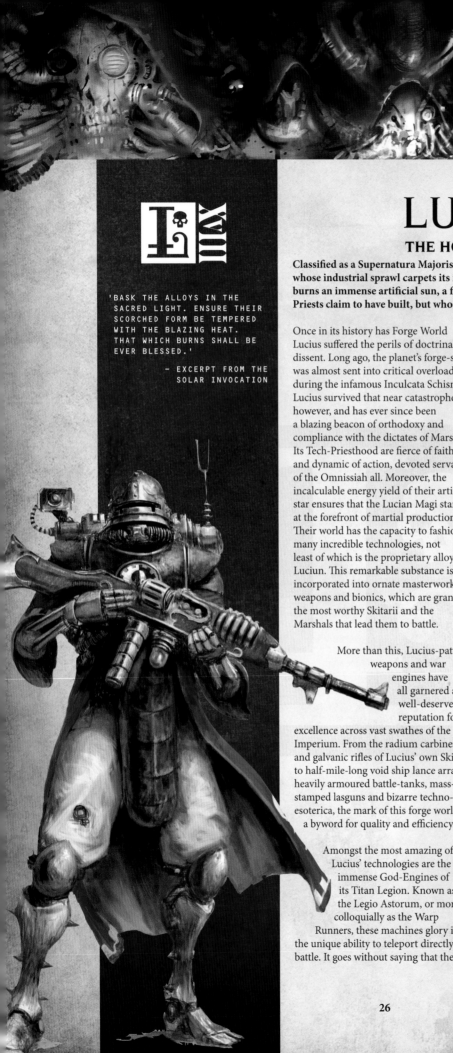

LUCIUS

THE HOLLOW FORGE

Classified as a Supernatura Majoris, the forge world of Lucius is vast, hollow planet whose industrial sprawl carpets its inner surfaces. In the planet's empty heart burns an immense artificial sun, a fusion mega-reactor that the Lucian Tech-Priests claim to have built, but whose origins may be more mysterious by far.

Once in its history has Forge World Lucius suffered the perils of doctrinal dissent. Long ago, the planet's forge-star was almost sent into critical overload during the infamous Inculcata Schism. Lucius survived that near catastrophe, however, and has ever since been a blazing beacon of orthodoxy and compliance with the dictates of Mars. Its Tech-Priesthood are fierce of faith and dynamic of action, devoted servants of the Omnissiah all. Moreover, the incalculable energy yield of their artificial star ensures that the Lucian Magi stand at the forefront of martial production. Their world has the capacity to fashion many incredible technologies, not least of which is the proprietary alloy Luciun. This remarkable substance is incorporated into ornate masterwork weapons and bionics, which are granted the most worthy Skitarii and the Marshals that lead them to battle.

More than this, Lucius-pattern weapons and war engines have all garnered a well-deserved reputation for excellence across vast swathes of the Imperium. From the radium carbines and galvanic rifles of Lucius' own Skitarii to half-mile-long void ship lance arrays, heavily armoured battle-tanks, mass-stamped lasguns and bizarre techno-esoterica, the mark of this forge world is a byword for quality and efficiency.

Amongst the most amazing of Lucius' technologies are the immense God-Engines of its Titan Legion. Known as the Legio Astorum, or more colloquially as the Warp Runners, these machines glory in the unique ability to teleport directly into battle. It goes without saying that the sudden appearance of towering engines of destruction upon the battlefield has won more than one battle in spectacular fashion, with weaker-willed foes fleeing in abject panic or dropping dead from terror before the Legio Astorum engines so much as open fire. Yet the Warp Runners are far from Lucius' only proud martial asset. Ever-eager to strike out into the galaxy and wrest from it the natural resources to feed the blessed forges, Lucius' macroclades are amongst the swiftest and most aggressive fielded by any forge world. Their Ironstriders, Serberys corps and Dunecrawlers surge towards the enemy with ferocious speed, often overrunning the enemy before they realise their peril.

The genius and innovation of the Tech-Priests of Lucius was displayed anew when a splinter fleet of Hive Fleet Leviathan invaded the planet. Despatching their Legio Cybernetica and a great host of battle servitors to the planet's outer surface, the Tech-Priests Dominus largely fought their battles from below the planet's crust. By tracking the motions of their servant clades and controlling activities via data-tethers, they waged their war without risking direct harm. Wherever the Tyranid swarms overcame their servitor armies, the Tech-Priests waited for the xenos predators to devour the meagre biological components before sending servo-skull swarms to carry the most vital of the remaining machine parts below the crust of the planet. There they were installed into fresh recruits, and the next wave sent back up to the surface. Though it took months to accomplish, the resultant war of attrition ended in victory. Deprived of biomatter, the Tyranid splinter fleet was forced to feed upon itself to generate replacement broods, and the xenos could not keep pace with the recycled machinery parts and refurbished robots.

AGRIPINAA

ORB OF A MILLION SCARS

Agripinaa is a world scarred by war, its legions forged in conflict's crucible and tempered through the fires of countless hellish battles. Long has this forge world resisted the hostile attentions of the Dark Gods' minions, for it stands perilously close to the warp maw known as the Eye of Terror.

Once, Agripinaa laboured day and night to supply the fortress world of Cadia with munitions for its endless vigil over the Eye of Terror. So integral to the forge world was that mission, that some Tech-Priests had interpreted the hermetic symbol in Agripinaa's heraldic iconography as representing the Cadian Gate standing supreme over the forces of Chaos. Cadia's fall has forced these and countless other assumptions to be rethought.

Even before Abaddon's victory during the Thirteenth Black Crusade, Agripinaa was already a heavily fortified and war-scarred world. Heretic raiding parties struck at the forge world often, some seeking to plunder its technological secrets while others hoped to disrupt the planet's crucial supply lines to key worlds throughout the Cadian war zone. Since Cadia's fall, the frequency and severity of those attacks has increased tenfold. Agripinaa exists in a state of near-constant conflict, fighting wars of both attack and defence as its macroclades seek to drive back the endless tide of foes spilling from the Eye of Terror. Typically dispassionate, the planet's Tech-Priests take every opportunity to hone their armies and defences both, dissecting every data psalm and noospheric inquisition extracted from each battle and employing their learnings with dogmatic determination. Yet the priests of the Omnissiah are not above emotion when pushed to it. The assaults upon their world by unclean servants of the Dark Mechanicum, by Obliterator Cults, acquisitive Warpsmiths and even loathsome Traitor Titan Legions have instilled in the Tech-Priests of Agripinaa a cold and unbending hatred for the worshippers of the Dark Gods. The priests have perfected countless methods of slaughtering their heretic foes, and will fight on against them even unto the

collapse of all logic and reason, such is their disgust.

While Agripinaa's stoic defenders have refined their protocols of repudiation and dogged resistance, its Tech-Priests have formulated complex strategies of aggressive counter-sieges as well. Huge wedges of Serberys Sulphurhounds are unleashed into advancing enemy formations in shockingly brutal and seemingly reckless manoeuvres. Smaller units of Skitarii Rangers and Serberys Raiders harry the enemy while flights of Archaeopter Fusilaves and Stratoraptors strike simultaneously, sometimes adding greatly to the forge world's own casualties. Any surviving Skitarii of the first charge are pulled back into the second wave, and then the procedure repeats. By the time the enemy reach the guns of the stationary defenders, they are fractured, bloodied and demoralised, their cohesion ready to fall when Agripinaa's precision volleys fall upon them.

As with many powerful and well-fortified worlds throughout the wider Cadian Gate, Agripinaa has become a focal point not only for conflict, but also for refugees. It is natural that fleeing Imperial citizens and soldiery alike would put aside their prejudices in such desperate times and seek shelter behind the ironclad bulwarks of the Adeptus Mechanicus. Agripinaa welcomes all willing to serve the Omnissiah. Many have chosen starvation over what the planet's Magi see as a logical contribution to ultimate victory, but countless others have stepped willingly into the Omnissiah's embrace. This influx of raw organic materials has thus far allowed Agripinaa to replace losses amongst its labour clades and Skitarii cohorts as swiftly as they are inflicted. Whether this will continue to be the case remains to be seen…

'THOU SHALT NOT SUFFER TO LIVE THOSE WHO PRACTISE AUTO-IDOLATRY OR FALSE WORSHIP OF ILLOGICAL DEITIES IN THE SIGHT OF THE OMNISSIAH. CLEANSE FOREVER THE GALACTIC NOOSPHERE OF THEIR DATACORROSIVE TAINT, AND THUS KNOW HIS BLESSING.'

– CATACHESIUM PRIMUS-ANALYTICUM INFINITUS, VERSE 126 TO THE 4TH POWER

STYGIES VIII
THE EVER STARING CYCLOPS

The Magi of Stygies VIII are not well-trusted by their peers from other forge worlds. Their Cohorts have a dark reputation for dubious behaviours relating to the pursuit and acquisition of proscribed xenos technologies, a practise about which their Tech-Priests remain secretive and singularly unrepentant.

'THOSE WHO DON THE BLINKERS OF WILFUL IGNORANCE MAY NO LONGER BEAR WITNESS TO THE TRUE ILLUMINATION OF THE OMNISSIAH. EVEN AMIDST THE DEEPEST SHADOWS, WE BATHE IN THAT HOLY LIGHT.'

– DAK-XXVII, CULAX BLACK GUARD

The forge world of Stygies VIII lies far to the galactic north of Terra. It is actually a moon, one of several orbiting a ringed gas giant in the binary star system of Vulcanis. Though the knowledge of the event is buried in the forge world's deepest and most ancient datastacks, this system was almost lost to heretic forces long ago, during the dark days of the Horus Heresy. As malevolent as the touch of the traitor might be, Stygies VIII was further tainted in that it was saved from conquest not by good, honest Imperial reinforcement, but by the pernicious activities of the Aeldari. None now live who know the truth of these events, for even Stygies VIII's Fabricator General is unaware of the hidden truth buried in the forge world's cogitational architecture. Yet though the root cause of xenos intervention might be lost, the effect of this strange interdiction can be seen in the secretive society known as the Xenarites who exist within the forge world's Tech-Priesthood.

The Xenarites study and seek to exploit all aspects of xenos technology. They court accusations of heresy by delving into the secret workings of everything from Drukhari shadow fields and T'au gravitic propulsion technologies to Chimeriac shivertech, Kinebrach spiteforging, Stryite barb-blades and countless other alien sciences besides. Ever-acquisitive, the armies of Stygies VIII have come into conflict many times with xenos races whose technologies they wish to appropriate; but also, on occasion, with Imperial forces who have either taken a dim view of the Xenarites' research, or else stood – knowingly or not – between the clandestine group and their prized knowledge. The more orthodox forces of the forge world are talented obfuscators as well, and their use of shrouding technologies, diversionary activities and secretive binharic sub-codes to conceal their labours has given the Tech-Priests of Stygies VIII a suspicious reputation indeed.

SEEKERS AFTER THE STONE

In recent centuries, the Xenarites have taken an interest in noctilith – known as blackstone throughout much of the Imperium. Noctilith is found upon many quarry worlds, scattered in strangely uniform deposits. Incredibly durable and remarkably ancient, blackstone can be either positively or negatively charged in relation to warp energies, effectively attracting or repelling them. While the utility of the substance appears obvious, the priests of most forge worlds have remained reticent to investigate so obviously alien a substance. The Xenarites have no such compunction. Thus, they were amongst the first to make the connection that noctilith is in fact a material first employed by the ancient galactic empire of the Necrons. As the rate of the aliens' revivification increases, more and more Necron tombs are awakening upon the same worlds where noctilith is found, rendering its acquisition ever more perilous. This has not dissuaded the legions of Stygies VIII, however. Many of their most recent campaigns have been waged in an effort to wrest vast blackstone deposits away from their ancient owners.

GRAIA

THE CROWN OF MIRACLES

The armed forces of forge world Graia are amongst the most indomitable, indefatigable and downright stubborn to fight in defence of the Imperium. They are a byword for martial discipline and obstinacy both, advancing into firestorms with inhuman fearlessness that is as unsettling as it is inspirational.

Everything about the armies of Graia bespeaks ironclad control. So hardwired is their logic it is said they can even shield themselves from the malign attentions of enemy psykers. Prior to entering battle, the ruling Tech-Priests of the Graian military draw up resilient battle plans and doctrinal subroutines based on dispassionate logic. These are then disseminated to their foot soldiers with the weight of holy writ. So commanded, every Graian warrior knows their role in the wider shape of the battle, and strives to fulfil it with unswerving determination.

Many are the eye-witness accounts from other Imperial forces of Graian Skitarii acting more like battle-automata than living, thinking beings. Neither terrifying inhuman enemies nor thunderous incoming fire can halt the warriors of Graia while their orders remain unfulfilled – indeed, their macroclades have been described as pressing forward unto their own destruction with an almost mindless determination. This tenacity has proven an asset upon many battlefields where Graian soldiery have crushed their foes under a relentless advance, or waged attritional battles that eventually broke the enemy with the horror of their cost. Yet it has also proven detrimental in battles such as the Ulgha Gulch Offensive and the Tsamuth Massacre where prudent retreat or rapid tactical flexibility would have prevented the wholesale annihilation of Graia's advancing cohorts. Of course, such tragic defeats carry little emotional weight with the forge world's Tech-Priests. Instead, each such disaster is simply analysed, dissected and broken down into strategic data which is fed into their predictive models for future conflicts.

Graia itself is unusual in that the forge world is crested by a geometrically perfect ring of space stations known as the Graian Crown. It is within this megastructure that the forge world's armies reside, and from it they deploy en masse to repel those who would seek to invade the world below. Moreover, the entire vast structure can move under its own power and even translate into warp space, allowing the armies of Graia to forge out across the galaxy and exploit the resources of distant worlds – though knowledge of this technology is suppressed as much as possible. Travel aboard the Graian Crown is an imperfect process; the megastructure has repeatedly attracted the hostile attentions of both warp entities and the ancient Necrons, and entire battles have been fought within its weirdly symmetrical depths to prevent it being overrun or captured. Yet so great an advantage is this immense battle-fortress that the logical value of its use to Graia far outweighs the potential risks of its loss to a hostile enemy force.

When the Graian Crown leaves its forge world, its fabrication temples are stocked with munitions and its holding decks provisioned with thousands of 'volunteers'. Once a suitable resource-rich world has been discovered, the Crown's chorazine shunt thrusters lock it into a stationary orbit like a tick. Fleets of industrial harvesters descend, leeching the world of its assets. Should an enemy be foolish enough to attempt to board the Crown, its production subroutines adapt. Hundreds of freshly built Skitarii and Servitors pour off the production line every minute, and servo carts deliver vast quantities of ammunition to the immoveable defenders. While the foe are being bled, the plunder of their world below continues unabated.

STEEL OF BODY, STEEL OF MIND. STEEL OF BODY, STEEL OF MIND. STEEL OF BODY, STEEL OF MIND. STEEL OF…

METALICA

THE GLEAMING GIANT OF ULTIMA SEGMENTUM

Metalica is a world sheathed entirely in adamantine, iron and steel. Its surface is covered with immense, interconnected industrial clusters and forge-shrines interspersed with landscapes of industrial waste. It is an unsleeping crucible of war production, whose polluted skies ring to the endless clangour of manufacture.

'IRON OVER FLESH, COGITATION OVER THOUGHT, INFORMATION OVER CONJECTURE. THUS IS PURITY, AND VICTORY, ASSURED.'

– FERROPSALM OF THE FABRICATOR GENERAL

Located deep within the Ultima Segmentum, forge world Metalica is the piston-driven industrial heart of the Charadon Sector. In a region located close to the ever-expanding Ork Empire of the Arch-Arsonist, and now also the raging fury of the Great Rift, the role of this world could not be more pivotal. Metalica's endless production quotas see dozens of war fronts kept supplied with arms and armour. Meanwhile, its renowned macroclades of Skitarii and Cohorts Cybernetica deploy with machine-like efficiency to crush threats both piratical and heretical throughout the entire region.

Such is the Metalican fervour for optimised industrial production, and their worship of mechanical sterility over organic impurity, that the forge world has been scoured of all native flora and fauna. Yet to think the planet lifeless would be an error – from pole to pole, Metalica seethes with indentured labour, dead-eyed servitors and conclaves of Tech-Priests avidly overseeing the production of yet more terrifying war engines and deadly weapons ready to fight in the Omnissiah's name. The cacophony of thundering pistons, roaring generatora, clattering assembly lines and endless binharic plainsong roll across

the artificial landscape like sonic tidal waves. The racket booms along ironclad canyons like the bellow of the Machine God himself. To the Metalican faithful, this endless industrial din is inspiring to the point of being transcendental, for it is the sound of their world worshipping the Omnissiah through deed and output both. They even ensure that it is echoed in the purposefully amplified blare of the weaponry and machines they employ; thus, every volley of fire or crushing armoured advance is a prayer to the Machine God writ large on the field of war.

Metalica stands proudly apart from Mars, both physically and doctrinally. The Metalican priesthood have long resisted any Martian attempts to impose remote rule. Thus, their Skitarii display only the barest amount of crimson within their heraldry, a grudging nod to the Red Planet that is all but drowned out amidst the white of Metalica. This colour is symbolic to the Metalicans as representative of the purity of the machine, and of its inevitable victory over weak organics. This striven-for purity has been tested as never before in recent times as Metalica has been imperilled by a Chaos invasion led by the Death Guard Traitor Legion.

THE IRON SKULLS

Forge world Metalica maintains its own Titan Legion. Formerly known as the Legio Metalica and, more recently, as the Iron Skulls, this august body was ravaged during the fighting on Armageddon. Under the careful leadership of Princeps Wynsten VanKassen they have gradually recovered their strength, yet in the bloody era of the Great Rift it seems all too likely that the legion has worse yet to endure.

RYZA

FURNACE OF SHACKLED STARS

Forge world Ryza is famed as the cradle from which many plasma-based weapons technologies have sprung. It is the originator of such wonders as the Stormblade, and the Leman Russ Executioner. Yet for all its magnificence and tech-heritage, Ryza is a world sorely embattled, caught amidst a storm of xenos foes.

From its thrumming forge-temples to its colossal ochre dust-dunes, its smog-thick skies and acidic rivers to its dense clouds of low-orbital industrial platforms, Ryza stands besieged. The greenskins of two vast Ork Waaagh!s have converged upon this forge world in their billions. Waaagh! Grax and Waaagh! Rarguts – either of which by themselves possess the sheer strength and weight of numbers in brutish warriors and war machines to overwhelm entire Imperial systems – pour down upon Ryza in endless waves. Savage greenskin techno-barbarians blast ancient and irreplaceable machineries to scrap, then add insult to injury by scavenging the wreckage in order to fashion ramshackle weapons of their own. Roaring with glee, hordes of Orks surge over the planet's surface in breakneck races and beat against the defences of each forge complex like the crashing waves of a bestial storm.

For all this, Ryza remains unbowed. If anything, the world's Tech-Priests could be accused of taking an unseemly delight in some aspects of their world's predicament. With the express permission of their world's Fabricator General, the priests of Ryza unleash the most potent weapons in their arsenals upon the invaders, treating each new engagement as a testing ground and gathering reams of combat data from victory and defeat alike. From macro-gatling lasers and plasma disintegration cannons to building-sized transdimensional beamers, anti-gravitic minefields, electrovoltaic blunderbusses and countless other martial esoterica, the priests of Ryza unleash endless terrifying weaponries against the Ork invaders. Of course, this has transformed the planet's surface into a hellish vision of total war. Yet neither the Ryzans themselves nor their greenskin foes appear perturbed by the nightmare they have created.

Nor does Ryza fight alone. Colossal Titans wade through the wreckage of blasted manufactora with guns thundering. Regiments of hard-bitten Catachan Imperial Guardsmen battle their alien foes through the toxic swamps of the Ryzan hinterlands. Through amassed martial might and ever-developing weaponry, the forge world continues to resist the overwhelming greenskin invasion. Though the battle still shows no end in sight, Ryza's commitments to other war zones remains undiminished, and they seek ever more diverse testing grounds for their protocols and materiel.

HONED BLADES

The Orks are too belligerent a threat ever to keep at arm's length forever. Thus, Ryzan Skitarii regularly find themselves facing their ferocious foes in close-quarters combat. This experience swiftly winnows those warriors who can hold their own in battle against hulking alien berzerkers from those who cannot. The forge world's priests view such battles as a chance to sharpen the collective blade of their Skitarii Cohorts, and their soldiery have developed a well-earned reputation for brutality in their own right.

'LET OUR ENEMIES COME. LET THEIR BLOOD BE THE UNGUENT THAT GREASES THE WHEELS OF OUR ENDLESS BLESSED ARTIFICE.'

– VANGUARD UNIT 09-TYBA, RADTAINMENT DIVISION

TRIPLEX PHALL

FORGE OF THE EASTERN FRONTIER

Triplex Phall is an isolationist forge world. Far from the cradle of Humanity, its Tech-Priests have developed secretive practices that have seen them withhold blessed blueprints even from holy Mars. This is made all the more noteworthy by the fact that the archeotechnological secrets of Triplex Phall are potent indeed.

The Tech-Priests of Triplex Phall rake over the most far-flung extremes of Human galactic settlement. They unearth long-lost worlds settled during Mankind's early expansion into the stars, and uncover secrets that predate even the Dark Age of Technology. Such remote delving has also brought the legions of Triplex Phall into contact with a number of lost Knight worlds, such as Grymm and Roland. These they have been swift to bring back into the Imperial fold, but also to bring first and foremost within their forge world's sphere of influence. Despite its remoteness, Triplex Phall's wealth of ancient tech-lore – which even includes several STC fragments unknown to outsiders– has made them a known name across the wider Imperium.

The Astra Militarum, in particular, has benefited from many Triplex Phall pattern arms and armour over the millennia.

For all this, the remote forge world's reticence to share their secrets has drawn the displeasure of Mars. In recent centuries, Martian legions have accompanied the Explorator fleets of Triplex Phall wherever they venture and flagged new discoveries to the Red Planet, lest they too vanish. Despite their invasive nature, these Martian reinforcements have proven fortuitous as – along with the lances of Triplex Phall's knightly vassals and the Titans of the Legio Victorum – they have helped to defend the remote forge world from repeated invasions and daemonic incursions.

DEIMOS

THE GIFT OF THE SIGILLITE

Upon the inception of the Grey Knights – the secret Chapter of Space Marines tasked with directly combating the daemonic threat – it was recognised that they would need their own forge world. Deimos is that forge world, and a more secretive or powerful sub-sect of the Adeptus Mechanicus it would be hard to find.

Deimos was once a moon of Mars. When the decision was made to provide the Grey Knights Chapter with their own dedicated forge world, potent technologies were used to spirit the moon away and relocate it in orbit above Titan, the Grey Knights' adopted home world. Since that time, the weapons required by the Emperor's daemon hunters have been produced within the manufactorums of Deimos. This includes standard Adeptus Astartes armaments as well as all the specialist gear required to combat warp-based foes, from psycannon ammunition to deadly psyk-out grenades. Each item receives psychic wards atop the blessings of the Omnissiah to ensure protection against daemonic taint. The handover of Deimos-forged wargear is carried out

by especially debilitated servitors whose scant minds and circuitry are scrubbed clean after each transaction. Such extreme measures ensure that the secrets of the Grey Knights can never be learned by the Tech-Priests – and conversely that the psychic Grey Knights cannot themselves glean any of the clandestine mysteries of the Adeptus Mechanicus.

Deimos is blessed with a great many macroclades, all bearing the triple-blessing of the Omnissiah. Additionally, three Knight houses are permanently stationed on Deimos, including House Steel, whose vows of silence in service to the Adeptus Mechanicus have lasted since the Great Crusade. Deimos' armies are used as guardians and procurement forces, and, upon request, march forth to battle alongside the Grey Knights.

VOSS PRIME

THE RIGHT HAND OF MARS

Reunited with Mars even before the Great Crusade, Voss prime is a forge world modelled after – and wholly loyal to – the Red Planet. The integrity and faith of the planet's Tech-Priests has never been in doubt, and neither has their exceptional materiel production rate, which is exceeded only by the Mars itself.

Voss Prime's constant and remarkable output of weaponry and war engines is owed in no small part to the forge world's merciless exploitation of the Mordon Belt. This vast swathe of asteroids has provided for Voss Prime even over the thousands of years that the forge world has existed, and still has not been exhausted. The countless rocky husks already mined hollow by the servitors of Voss Prime have been repurposed as defensive emplacements – some autonomous, some manned – to create an incredibly potent defensive barrier around the forge world. When coupled with Voss Prime's ability to deploy vast numbers of superior armoured fighting vehicles and Legio Cybernetica battle robots, these defences have proven sufficient to see off countless invasions by xenos hordes, heretical raiders and even a nightmarish daemonic incursion. Although some of the most profitable of the Mordon Belt's asteroids have been mined dry, opportunity for seemly expansion has arisen with the Indomitus Crusade, and Voss Prime has unleashed huge armies with the intention of securing new asset streams at any cost.

If there is a weak point in Voss Prime's armour, it is that their plasma weaponry has never been as reliable nor as effective as that produced by other forge worlds. That they have not asked for aid in rectifying this issue, and that it has not been offered even by their close ally Mars, is indicative of the pride and secrecy that exists even amongst the most devout of the Cult Mechanicus.

GRYPHONNE IV

THE LOST FORGE

The tale of Gryphonne IV is a caution against the prideful and stubborn tendencies of the Cult Mechanicus. Yet this is a warning almost wholly unheeded, even by those of the forge world's legions who escaped its doom, and who still seek a new planet upon which to rebuild their technological empire.

Gryphonne IV was long a name associated with industrial grandeur and implacable martial conquest. Enduring alone through the nightmarish Age of Strife, Gryphonne IV was eventually rediscovered by the Great Crusade and brought back into the Imperial fold with much honour and glory. The legions of this forge world only built upon their hallowed reputation as the centuries passed, marching resolutely to battle alongside the armies of the Imperium and crushing entire worlds beneath the tread of the God-Engines of Legio Gryphonicus. The forge world ruled its own not-inconsiderable empire of eight entire star systems, known as the Gryphonne Octad, and it drew from them the vast material wealth that only rendered the forge world ever mightier.

It was the alien scourge of the Tyranids that finally laid Gryphonne IV low. Hive Fleet Leviathan descended upon the Gryphonne Octad, and rather than relocating their facilities and abandoning their empire, the Tech-Priests of Gryphonne IV elected to stand their ground. Their certainty in their own invulnerability endured even as their guns were silenced and their legions devoured, their Titans dragged down by the endless swarms and their forge temples overrun. Only in the last desperate hours did a handful of Tech-Priests escape the doom of their world, fleeing along with their Skitarii and all the precious datastacks they could salvage.

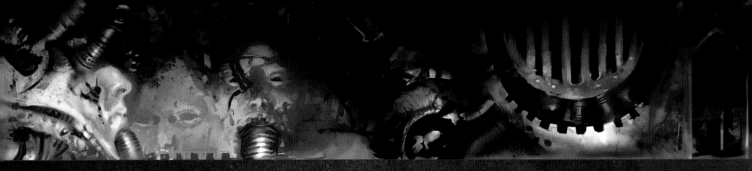

The Aeldari's head snapped back, its neck breaking, as the shot burned away the creature's potential energies in a single, lethal instant. The xenos spasmed as it fell to the ground, kicking up handfuls of bright silica sand. The three Aeldari alongside it reacted instantly, but Py-lex 422's squadron had already let fly, and six more thuds were followed by crackles of flaring energy, cracking armour and flinging the aliens like thin marionettes over the dry dunes.

Already moving while the corpses still twitched, Py-lex 422 meticulously thanked the machine spirit of his galvanic carbine, noting with satisfaction the synchronous movement as his five Raiders did likewise. Their movements were practised and precise, calculated to draw as little attention as possible. The squadron advanced from their opportunistic firing position, obscured from enemy retaliation by spear-like upthrusts of pale rock through which their mounts wove. Two of their cybercanids were restless, he noticed, straining at fleeting target acquisitions their sensors suites were detecting, but these additional movements were within Py-lex 422's tolerance parameters. It was expected. Their two riders had only recently been promoted to the Serberys corps. It would take this holy campaign to see them fully bond with their complex mounts of plasteel, neo-bronze, ebonite, oiled leather and sigil-carved plutonic cores. The Raider Alpha never failed to marvel in awe at the spirit that had been granted to cold iron – granted through the power of the Omnissiah, and directed through his humble vessel, Magos Kyberian.

As if summoned by the thought, an angelic chime sounded in Py-lex 422's iron-bound cranium. The Magos' previously issued protocol reinforced itself upon his consciousness, its scripture updating as data scrolled past his mind's eye.

++Primary protocol > reacquiring target: signal intermittent: commit to immediate re-evaluation of zone delta-rho 33.190z++

The true quarry was still out there, having threaded back within the xenos lines. That will not save you, Py-lex 422 vowed. Sending an impulse to his steed, he led Squadron Thoreta-Pentus in a stealthy run towards the indicated hunting zone, slipping through the spears of rock as they skirted the open terrain to their left. This pristine basin would soon be churned by the righteous footfalls of the rest of his cohort, ground and pounded into an oily, bloody quagmire according to schedule. The Machine God would not be denied its prize of this world, but its acquisition must be a declaration of unambiguous intent and absolute conviction. The xenos were faithless and slippery, fighting against fate and logic, and a feral band of ghost-like saboteurs and assassins had struck at the cohort from inconsistent angles with filthy, tainted weapons twisted out of holy norm. Py-lex 422's cortical augmentations flared with anger at the thought of the Machine God's chosen cut down and ancient relics destroyed. Now, Mars hunted these unenlightened heathens in turn, and Py-lex 422 was their relentless pursuer – a tool of divine vengeance.

From behind them where the Martian front advanced, the Alpha detected the distinctive, chattering frequency of radium carbines and the whine of arcing belleros projectiles followed by explosions of spectroscopic energy. He issued a rapid, binharic hymnal through the noospheric connection with his mount, beseeching its predatory machine spirit to modulate its footfalls to match the detonations. He signalled the rest of the squadron through their encrypted cohort-specific data-net to do likewise. Gant 6-Beta, his experienced second-in-command, submitted a query. Py-lex 422, shook his head as he replied, his cybercanid's steel skull echoing his movements.

'Negative, 6-Beta. The Omnissiah has not yet bestowed the target's location. He invites us to prove our worth in obtaining such knowledge for ourselves.'

Having penetrated the enemy lines and eliminated the advance guard, the Raiders swiftly prowled through zone delta-rho 33.190z. Their search pattern alternated at varying, predetermined intervals to wrong-foot their quarry, combing the undulating and rock-strewn terrain that lay hazed with smoke, fumes and wisps of sacred incense blowing from the advancing Skitarii lines. The fearsome muzzles of the Raiders' mounts hung low, sweeping from side to side, the riders' ebonite and bronze carbines following their gaze as though physically connected. The cybercanids' ocular arrays focussed and filtered, switching through dozens of different energy readings per second, while olfac sensors, microseismic detectors and tympanoscopes gorged on thousands more sensory inputs. The corps knew this multispectrum suite as the Eye of Serberys, and through it Py-lex 422 and his squadron perceived the hunt zone in a wash of sacred data.

Omnissiah, grant us the wisdom to perceive that which you would reveal, he silently intoned. Py-lex 422 briefly raised his head to the skies, his cybercanid's enhanced vision

drawn upward by the movement. In that moment, he not only witnessed the radiant, winking sigils that marked the glorious fleet assets in orbit – every nuance of their projected course laid out, every scrap of authorised data circling them like haloes – he could feel their beneficence reaching out to him. The warmth of the Magos' enlightened wisdom stretched out and touched his mind. In an instant, the cogitative functions of Squadron Thoreta-Pentus were sharpened, and Py-lex 422 felt the Machine God sweep aside irrelevant data-streams.

++Primary protocol > reacquiring target: signal-gheists multiplying > correcting: increase evaluation of zone delta-rho 33.190z > sextant 5-7++

Gant 6-Beta was the first to acquire minute empyric anomalies, fluctuating warp signatures like the scattered afterglow of a teleportarium activation. Magos Kyberian's meditations had determined these irregularities to be the heretical footsteps of these xenos. Such trails had been impossible to track with certainty from orbit, and only the expertise of the fleet's Raiders had been counted upon to sniff them out. The data was parsed and distributed to the squadron in a moment. Now that an identifiable spoor had been locked onto, the eager cybercanids increased their pace. They did so individually, at varying rates, careful to avoid the sudden change of speed and direction that would give to their quarry any warning of impending doom.

The trace appeared random and inconstant; vanishing and returning as if untethered in time. *Dabblers in witchery*, Py-lex 422 inwardly sneered. *The warp's mysteries are the sovereign property of the Machine God and his most trusted priests. How dare such filth believe they can understand it!*

More evidence poured into the shared noospheric link between the cybercanids and their riders. Subtly disturbed sand dunes and microvortices of displaced air in the presence of the warp anomalies increased, their coincidence irrefutable. *We're closing on them.*

An aggressive warning chime suddenly spiked through the complex mesh of data Py-lex 422 was instinctively processing: *enemy movement detected, fourth quadrant, threat probability 87.8%*. His mount's passive augurs suddenly took over, feeding the Alpha a barrage of tactical information. Py-lex 422 swivelled in his mag-locked saddle, assessing range and elevation through his mount's eyes, and unleashing a flurry of shots all within a fraction of a second.

His consciousness now caught up, processing the input. Squadron Thoreta-Pentus banked fluidly towards the enemy's position, accelerating into a loping run. Flickering shimmers rent the air ahead of them, first on one heading, then another. Heavily armoured Aeldari appeared to coalesce out of thin air. Despite bearing some kind of huge backpack, they ran swiftly, firing without pause before leaping through suddenly yawning portals that swallowed them again. The xenos reappeared instantly at a distance, dashing onwards in seemingly random headings. Rolling with their mounts' rapid changes of direction, Py-lex 422's Raiders unleashed a storm of carbine fire, pouring shots into the Aeldari as they appeared, trying to pin down the apparitions as they ran between ghost-like vanishings, attempting to predict their re-entry points.

The xenos fired flurries of mist-like shots as they fled. One experienced Raider lost a leg, her binharic cry of anger and loss flaring through the squadron's data-net. On the xenos' next appearance, one of Py-lex 422's new recruits was hit full on. A cloud of monomolecular wire wrapped around the Raider's flailing arms and the cybercanid's kicking limbs as blood, sacred oils and blessed promethium fountained from a hundred open gashes.

Wedded to Py-lex 422's instincts, the enhanced tracking wetware of the Eye of Serberys began to predict likely trajectories for the enemies, narrowing intercept angles and calculating probability matrices. Overlaid before the Alpha's vision was a rapidly diminishing number of glowing parabola, the combination of the squadron's gestalt experience and cogitative networking paring the options down until only one remained. Squadron Thoreta-Pentus raced forward, ready to pounce.

At that moment, Magos Kyberian delivered the word of the Machine God, speaking with the Omnissiah's awesome power directly to each warrior. The remnants of Py-lex 422's hindbrain forced him to gasp, his mechanical lungs heaving with sublime adoration. Almost without knowing it, the Alpha drew an electoo-inscribed sabre from his scabbard, as his Raiders did likewise. The xenos jumped from the immaterium before them, exposed and unable to flee in time and Py-lex 422 led his squadron into the fray. His emitters unleashed a binharic roar of praise as Squadron Thoreta-Pentus leapt crashing into the creatures, heavy sabres aimed for their alien hearts.

ILLUMINATUM MECHANICUS

One who looks for consistency in Skitarii augmentations would be disappointed. A soldier of the Adeptus Mechanicus may have a punchcard skullslot and leather bellows for lungs, whilst at the same time housing quantum bioware in their brain. Their Tech-Priest masters bear far more ostentatious enhancements, limited only by their individual power and eccentricity. Yet those bound to the same forge world employ traditional hues and iconography that mark them as part of the same holy endeavour.

The warriors of the Skitarii Legions bear the colours of their forge world on their heavy robes. Many forge worlds include the traditional red of Mars among their livery, as a way of acknowledging the primacy of the Red Planet, though some minimise its inclusion or reject it altogether in ancient displays of autonomy. The construction, materials and patina of the warriors' augmentations can also be a historic means of identity, for forge worlds pride themselves on the distinctive quality of their fabrications.

Adorning the hems of robes and sculpted chest plates of the Skitarii are ancient symbols and icons, each one sacred to the Cult of the Machine God – most notable among them the skull and cog that represents the Adeptus Mechanicus throughout the Imperium. Numerals, graphemes and sigils identify a warrior's position in the byzantine hierarchy of their forge world, and these are also applied to the flanks of war engines or implanted as glowing electoos. Battle Maniples of Skitarii infantry typically comprise six squads. Three maniples in varying combinations comprise a War Cohort, and above these are macroclades formed of four cohorts, resulting in twelve maniples per macroclade – twelve being a sacred number to the Adeptus Mechanicus. Specialist, sometimes temporary, formations are also raised, such as Infiltration Clades, Armoured Cohorts and Close Assault Maniples.

Squad Markings

Skitarii infantry bear the sigil of their forge world and their individual squad number upon their robes.

42   9¥   4Þ   16

These squad markings hail from Mars, the senior forge world employing the skull and cog as its sigil.

Skitarii Vanguard with plasma caliver

Skitarii Vanguard with radium carbine

Skitarii Vanguard Alpha with arc pistol and power sword

Skitarii Ranger Alpha with phosphor blast pistol and power maul

Skitarii Ranger with arc rifle

Skitarii Ranger with galvanic rifle and enhanced data-tether

Sigils

Arcane sigils identifying the unit's maniple may be borne by a unit's Alpha or Princeps, their overseer status denoted with a skull.

Δ   Σ   Ω

Maniple sigils

16^Δ   34^Σ   4ß^Ω

Unit leader markings

36

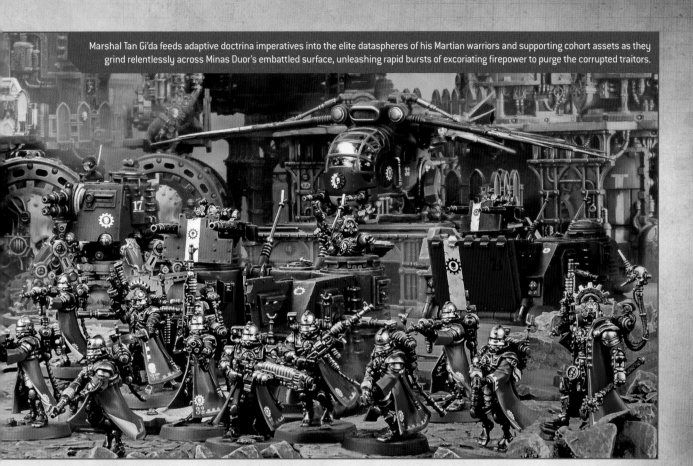

Marshal Tan Gi'da feeds adaptive doctrina imperatives into the elite dataspheres of his Martian warriors and supporting cohort assets as they grind relentlessly across Minas Duor's embattled surface, unleashing rapid bursts of excoriating firepower to purge the corrupted traitors.

In an aural and neural barrage of disruptive frequencies, sinister cyborgs of Metalica's Sicaran Clades ambush their reeling greenskin prey. Reinforcements arrive via Archaeopter Transvector to complete the purifying eradication of these blasphemous tech-looters.

Mars' incessant delving for arcana stirs up mutated strains of xenos cultists. The brood coven has staked its claim over Fordhrast IX, adamant its claws are sunk deeply enough into the world, but they have not compensated for the acquisitive zeal of the Machine God's chosen.

Sulphurhounds and Raiders
The cavalry squadrons of the Serberys Corps may bear expanded squad markings that denote specialist subdivisions.

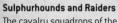

The elite of the Skitarii bear the highest quality augmentations. 💀

Serberys Sulphurhound with two phosphor pistols

Serberys Sulphurhound Alpha with phosphor blast pistol and arc maul

Serberys Raider with galvanic carbine

The treacherous terrain of the Rhekspine Ridge is no impediment to Unit Lhemda 31-2's cybercanids. Mag-locked in their saddles, the Raiders unleash furious volleys, sending the lifeless bodies of Ork infiltrators plummeting thousands of feet.

Fulgurite Electro-Priest with
electroleech stave

Corpuscarii Electro-Priest with electrostatic gauntlets

Kataphron Breacher with heavy arc rifle and arc claw

Kataphron Destroyer with heavy grav-cannon and
phosphor blaster

Kastelan Robot with incendine combustor and
Kastelan phosphor blasters

Kastelan Robot with incendine combustor and
Kastelan fists

Deep below the surface of a Stilled world in the Pariah Nexus, fanatical Electro-Priests of the Fulgurite order discover the troglodytic hoarders of the planet's Motive Force. The sightless Priests need only the illumination of faith to crush the Necrons skulls and leech their vital essence.

The Host Robotic of the Sentinel Cohort advance with pre-programmed tactical precision, ready to obey the directive to wade into the Tyranid swarm head-on. Broken and incinerated broods by the score already mark the relentless passage over Trecuithna's semi-digested surface.

Archmagos Dominus Belisarius Cawl

Tech-Priest Manipulus with magnarail
lance and Omnissian staff

Tech-Priest Dominus Shivan Lem calibrates his hatred for the witch-breed xenos, allowing it to bleed into his wide-broadcast canticles and the
aggressive imperatives. The devoted of Ryza tear towards the Aeldari with the pure logic of savage unmaking prioritising their actions.

Beset by Necrons, Belisarius Cawl demands the industrial facilities of his orbital-dropped acquisitorum be brought online immediately. He cants a blurted vow that the treasures he seeks are his alone, as he pours his directives into his minions and unleashes his esoteric arsenal.

Skitarii Vanguard of
Stygies VIII

Skitarii Ranger of
Stygies VIII

Kataphron Breacher of
Metalica

Tech-Priest Enginseer of
Voss Prime

Corpuscarii Electro-Priest
of Ryza

Tech-Priest Enginseer of
Triplex Phall

THE RULES

Welcome to the rules section of *Codex: Adeptus Mechanicus*. On the following pages you will find all the rules content you need to bring every aspect of the Adeptus Mechanicus Forge Worlds to life on your tabletop battlefields. Maybe you're inspired to dive straight into some open play games, maybe you want to shape your own tales of glory and infamy with narrative play, or perhaps you can't wait to pit yourself against your opponents in nail-biting matched play contests. Whichever appeals to you – even if it's a bit of all three – this section of your Codex provides a modular toolbox that allows you to get the most out of your collection.

Of course, there's no need to take it all in at once! Some of the content on the following pages – things like your army's datasheets and the rules for its weapons – will be useful no matter what kind of game you're playing. Others, such as your army's Stratagems, Warlord Traits and Relics, will become relevant once you start playing games with Battle-forged armies. Then there's content like Holy Orders that you will unlock by including particular models in your tabletop army. You can include such new elements at your own pace; whether you're a brand new hobbyist playing your first few games or a veteran general ready to cause carnage, there's plenty here to provide you with countless hours of fresh and exciting gameplay.

On top of this, the Adeptus Mechanicus are the only faction in Warhammer 40,000 with access to the Canticles of the Omnissiah and Doctrina Imperatives rules, through which you can adapt and overcome your foes using machine might and religious fervour. You will find everything you need on the following pages to include these rules in your games of Warhammer 40,000, not to mention bespoke content for your Adeptus Mechanicus force, including a system allowing you to build your own custom archeotech weapons from scratch!

'The Tech-Priests of Delphi are very special customers. There are few out here on the Eastern Fringe to whom one can safely pass strange items with little questioning. I have never dealt directly with any of their triumvirate of Fabricators General – the so-called 'Charities of Delphi' – but their discretion runs as deeply as their appreciation for my expert eye. Their goodwill in the form of excellent repairs and generous refuelling every time I happen to call is, indeed, charitable. Truly, the forge world's masters – Lady Euphrosinn, Lady Thilya and Lady Agaeleatrix – are wise. Exactly how they appear to know when my contacts have some unusual treasure is something that has proven impossible to establish so far.'

- *Rogue Trader Vileth Rey Aggranoza*

BATTLE-FORGED RULES

DETACHMENT ABILITIES (PG 49-59)
Units in Adeptus Mechanicus Detachments gain additional abilities to better reflect how their armies operate together and wage war on the battlefield. You can find out more about. Detachment abilities in the Battle-forged Armies section of the Warhammer 40,000 Core Book.

STRATAGEMS (PG 60-63)
Adeptus Mechanicus armies have access to unique battlefield strategies and tactics that they can utilise to best their foes in any theatre of war; these are represented by the Stratagems in this section, which you can spend Command points to use in your games. You can find out more about Stratagems and Command points in the Warhammer 40,000 Core Book.

HOLY ORDERS (PG 64-65)
Tech-Priest models in your Adeptus Mechanicus army can be upgraded to gain new abilities based on the Holy Orders of the Adeptus Mechanicus, each adhering to their own code of war and priorities.

ARMY RULES

WARLORD TRAITS (PG 66-67)
The Warlord of an Adeptus Mechanicus army can have one of the traits presented in this section. These help to personalise the leader of your force and better reflect their individual combat prowess and command style on the battlefield.

RELICS (PG 68-69)
Adeptus Mechanicus characters can take powerful artefacts and ancient weapons called Relics into battle; these Relics and the rules they bestow are described in this section.

MATCHED PLAY RULES

CHAPTER APPROVED RULES (PG 70)
If you are playing a battle that instructs you to select secondary objectives, then you will be able to choose from the Adeptus Mechanicus ones printed here that represent tactical goals unique to their armies. You can find out more about selecting secondary objectives in many matched play mission packs, including the Eternal War mission pack found in the Warhammer 40,000 Core Book.

CRUSADE RULES

CRUSADE (PG 72-83)
Adeptus Mechanicus have access to a host of additional rules that enhance your Crusade experience and further personalise your Crusade force. These include bespoke Agendas, Requisitions, Battle Traits and Crusade Relics that reflect the rich background of Adeptus Mechanicus armies. Amongst the rules presented in this section are Archeotech Treasures, a brand new type of wargear that the Tech-Priests of the Adeptus Mechanicus can seek out and construct themselves.

DATASHEETS

DATASHEETS (PG 84-111)
This section is essential to all Adeptus Mechanicus players, regardless of preferred play style, containing as it does the datasheets for Adeptus Mechanicus units. Each datasheet describes, among other things, the profiles of its models, the wargear they can be equipped with and the abilities they have. You can find out more about datasheets in the Warhammer 40,000 Core Book.

WARGEAR

WEAPON PROFILES (PG 112-115)
This section provides an alphabetised list of all the weapons that Adeptus Mechanicus units can be equipped with, and should be used in conjunction with the datasheets section.

POINTS

POINTS VALUES (PG 116-117)
If you are playing a game that uses points values, you can use the alphabetised lists in this section to determine the cost of each unit from your army. These values will be reviewed and updated annually.

RULES REFERENCE

GLOSSARY (PG 119)
In this section you will find a glossary of rules terms used in this Codex. This is intended to work alongside the glossary found in the Warhammer 40,000 Core Book, and aid in resolving any complex rules interactions that may arise.

REFERENCE (PG 120)
Here you will find a handy bullet-pointed rules reference that summarises some common Adeptus Mechanicus rules.

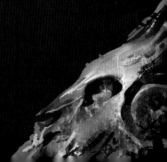

COMBAT PATROL

Combat Patrol is the smallest size game, and the Adeptus Mechanicus force below is a great way to start – regardless of whether you want to play an open play game, forge a narrative with a Crusade army, or compete in a matched play mission. Created from the contents of the Adeptus Mechanicus Combat Patrol boxed set, this force can be used in a Battle-forged army, and in itself comprises a Patrol Detachment, as described in the Warhammer 40,000 Core Book.

The Skitarii Rangers are a reliable unit that, as part of a Battle-forged army, gain the Objective Secured ability (see the Warhammer 40,000 Core Book), making them ideally suited to holding battlefield

objectives. Their powerful galvanic rifles and long range transuranic arquebus allow them to reach out and touch large portions of the battlefield with their ranged firepower.

The Kataphron Destroyers, meanwhile, provide the muscle to back up the Skitarii Rangers. Their tough, durable chassis allow them to weather the enemy's attacks and keep on fighting. The Heavy Battle Servitor ability also allows them to push forwards, taking mid-field objectives while still delivering a devastating barrage from their own Heavy weapons.

The Onager Dunecrawler is the heavy hitter of the force, its wide array of guns

and missiles able to blast apart both heavy armour and infantry alike, – although it is particularly adept against any enemy aircraft that might be foolish enough to engage it.

The Tech-Priest Enginseer is a key support character in this army, able to repair the Onager Dunecrawler and power up its weaponry, while also giving the Skitarii Rangers access to their unique Doctrina Imperatives – allowing them to respond to any number of varied threats on the battlefield.

DETACHMENT ABILITIES

An **Adeptus Mechanicus** Detachment is one that only includes models with the **Adeptus Mechanicus** keyword (excluding models with the **Agent of the Imperium** or **Unaligned** keyword).

- **Adeptus Mechanicus** Detachments gain the Forge World Dogmas ability.

- **Adeptus Mechanicus** Detachments (excluding Auxiliary Support Detachments) gain the Knight of the Cog ability.

- Troops units in **Adeptus Mechanicus** Detachments gain the Objective Secured ability (this ability is described in the Warhammer 40,000 Core Book).

FORGE WORLD DOGMAS

Each Forge World has its own combat philosophy suited to the skills of its warriors.

All **Adeptus Mechanicus** units (other than **Servitors** units) with this ability, and all the models in them, gain a dogma so long as every unit in their Detachment is from the same Forge World. The dogma gained depends upon which Forge World they are from, as shown on the following pages.

Example: A Graia unit with the Forge World Dogmas ability gains the Refusal to Yield dogma.

If your Forge World does not have an associated dogma, you must instead create a new dogma for them, as described on pages 58-59. This allows you to customise the rules for your Forge World to best represent their fighting style.

In either case, write down all of your Detachments' dogmas on your army roster.

KNIGHT OF THE COG

For each Detachment in your army with this ability, you can select one **Questor Mechanicus** Super-heavy Auxiliary Detachment in your army. Models in that Detachment gain the **Knight of the Cog** keyword.

ETERNAL VIGILANCE IS THE DUTY OF ALL THE MACHINE GOD'S SERVANTS. THUS DO THE SKITARII HAVE THEIR EYELIDS REMOVED UPON INCEPTION, THAT THEY MIGHT BEHOLD THE OMNISSIAH'S WORKS UNTIL THE DAY THEIR SERVITUDE IS ENDED.

FORGE WORLDS

BATTLE-FORGED RULES

If your army is Battle-forged, **<Forge World>** units in **Adeptus Mechanicus** Detachments gain access to the following Forge World rules, provided every model in that Detachment that is drawn from a Forge World is from the same Forge World. Such a Detachment is referred to as a Forge World Detachment.

WARLORD TRAITS

Each Forge World has an associated Forge World Warlord Trait. If an **Adeptus Mechanicus <Forge World> Tech-Priest Character** model gains a Warlord Trait, they can have the relevant Forge World Warlord Trait instead of a Warlord Trait from pages 66-67.

STRATAGEMS

Each Forge World has an associated Forge World Stratagem. If your army includes a Forge World Detachment (excluding Auxiliary Support, Super-heavy Auxiliary or Fortification Network Detachments), then you will gain access to the relevant Forge World Stratagem.

ARCANA MECHANICUM

Each Forge World has an associated Forge World Arcana Mechanicum. If your army is led by an **Adeptus Mechanicus <Forge World> Warlord**, you can give the relevant Forge World Arcana Mechanicum to an **Adeptus Mechanicus <Forge World> Character** model in your army instead of giving them an Arcana Mechanicum Relic from pages 68-69. Named characters (such as Belisarius Cawl) cannot be given an Arcana Mechanicum Relic.

Note that some Relics replace one of the model's existing items of wargear. Where this is the case, you must, if you are using points values, still pay the cost of the wargear that is being replaced. Write down any Arcana Mechanicum Relics your models have on your army roster.

*Example: A Battle-forged army includes an **Adeptus Mechanicus** Detachment in which every unit has the **Mars** keyword. A **Character** model in that Detachment that is given a Warlord Trait can instead be given the Panegyric Procession Warlord Trait. You also have access to the Wrath of Mars Stratagem and can spend CPs to use it, and if the army's **Warlord** is selected from this Detachment, then a **Mars Character** model in your army that could be given an Arcana Mechanicum Relic can instead be given The Red Axe.*

MARS

The Tech-Priests of Mars rigidly believe in their blessed superiority in the eyes of the Machine God, and in the holy perfection of their armies.

DOGMA: MASTERS OF THE FORGE

The favour of the Machine God can be seen in the powerful optimisation granted by every static-ridden psalm incanted by his most faithful followers. This is manifest also in Mars' ultimate mastery of manufacture and the excellence of its craftsmanship.

- **Skitarii** units with this dogma gain the Canticles of the Omnissiah ability (pg 84-85).
- Each time a unit with this dogma is selected to shoot or fight, you can re-roll one hit roll when resolving that unit's attacks.

WARLORD TRAIT: PANEGYRIC PROCESSION

The Tech-Priests of the Red Planet lead their disciples in a synchronous cortege of war.

In your Command phase, you can select one friendly **Mars Cult Mechanicus Core** unit within 6" of this **Warlord**. If you do so, then select one Canticle (pg 85) – this can be one that has already been active for your army. Until the start of your next Command phase, both this **Warlord** and that unit benefit from the selected Canticle instead of the one that is active for your army.

ARCANA MECHANICUM: THE RED AXE

A colossal, cog-bladed axe edged in priceless starmetal and emitting a crimson glow, the appropriately named Red Axe is a fabled treasure from the war vaults of Mars. The supply of this unique ore is so limited that only one such weapon has ever been created, and it is claimed that few foes can withstand its blow.

Mars model equipped with an Omnissian axe only. This Relic replaces an Omnissian axe and has the following profile:

WEAPON	RANGE	TYPE	S	AP	D
The Red Axe	Melee	Melee	+2	-5	2

Abilities: Each time the bearer fights, it makes 3 additional attacks with this weapon.

WRATH OF MARS	1CP/2CP

Mars – Battle Tactic Stratagem

None can smite the blasphemer like those from Mars, for theirs is the most righteous of zeal. All praise the glory of the Machine God!

Use this Stratagem in your Shooting phase, when a **Mars** unit is selected to shoot. Until the end of the phase, each time a model in that unit makes an attack, an unmodified wound roll of 6 inflicts 1 mortal wound on the target in addition to any normal damage (to a maximum of 6 mortal wounds).

If that unit has a Power Rating of 11 or more, this Stratagem costs 2CP; otherwise, it costs 1CP.

mARS41

THE GRINDING OF WAR'S GEARS IS A SYMPHONY OF PRAISE TO THE OMNISSIAH, FUELLED WITH BLOOD AND OILED WITH DEVOTION.

FORGE WORLDS

LUCIUS

Lucius employs many materials and technologies virtually unknown on other forge worlds, an advantage it jealously guards. The Hollow Forge craves ever more resources and it unleashes armies of acquisition in a never-ending stream.

DOGMA: SOLAR BLESSING

Lucius is renowned for its craftsmanship and unique solar-blessed ores, often marked by the ritual scorching of its titanic forges.

- Each time an attack with a Damage characteristic of 1 is allocated to a model with this dogma, add 1 to any armour saving throw made against that attack.
- Add 3" to the Range characteristic of ranged weapons that models with this dogma are equipped with.

WARLORD TRAIT: LUMINESCENT BLESSING

As the priestly rulers of Lucius recite their dazzling consecration, energy is redirected to infuse their masterwork alloys creating a halo of divine defence.

In your Command phase, select one **Lucius Core** unit within 9" of this **Warlord**. Until the start of your next Command phase, each time an attack is made against that unit, an unmodified wound roll of 1-3 for that attack fails, irrespective of any abilities that the weapon or the model making the attack may have.

ARCANA MECHANICUM: THE SOLAR FLARE

The Solar Flare is a unique Lucius invention – a personal teleportation device that causes the bearer to burst from the warp in a flash of blinding white light.

Lucius model only. Once per battle, in your Movement phase, the bearer can use this Relic. If it does so, the bearer's unit and up to one friendly **Lucius Core** unit within 3" of the bearer can be removed from the battlefield and set back up anywhere on the battlefield that is more than 9" away from any enemy models. If two units are set back up on the battlefield using this Relic, both units must be placed wholly within 6" of each other.

LEGIO TELEPORTARIUM   **1CP**

Lucius – Wargear Stratagem

The Tech-Priests of Lucius apply the same technologies they use to shift Titans through the warp to master battlefield teleportation.

Use this Stratagem before the battle, during the Declare Reserves and Transports step (if you are playing a mission without this step, use this Stratagem during deployment instead). Select one **Lucius** unit (excluding **Vehicle** units) from your army. You can set up that unit in a teleportarium instead of setting it up on the battlefield. If you do so, then in the Reinforcements step of one of your Movement phases, you can set up that unit anywhere on the battlefield that is more than 9" away from any enemy models. You can only use this Stratagem once, unless you are playing a Strike Force battle (in which case you can use this Stratagem twice), or an Onslaught battle (in which case you can use this Stratagem three times).

THE ILLUMINATED LETTER THAT FORMS LUCIUS' ICON IS BURNT INTO THE PLANET'S SURFACE, EACH DETAIL A DOZEN MILES FROM TOP TO BOTTOM.

AGRIPINAA

Embroiled in constant war near the Eye of Terror, Agripinaa's armies stand as immovable bastions of the Omnissiah's will.

DOGMA: STAUNCH DEFENDERS

With imperatives refined over countless horrific close assaults, those of Agripinaa retain a cast-iron composure in the face of advancing foes.

- Each time a model with this dogma makes a ranged attack that targets a unit within half range, the Armour Penetration characteristic of that attack is improved by 1.
- Each time an enemy unit declares a charge against a unit with this dogma, if this unit is not within Engagement Range of any enemy units, it can Hold Steady or Set to Defend.

WARLORD TRAIT: VERSE OF VENGEANCE

Rousing code in binharic duometer incites fury for the lost worlds around Agripinaa, the devoted extending their functions for one last act of retribution.

In your Command phase, select one friendly **Agripinaa Core** unit within 6" of this **Warlord**. Each time a model in that unit is destroyed by an attack made by an enemy model, roll one D6: on a 4+, do not remove the destroyed model from play – it can, after the attacking model's unit has finished making its attacks, either shoot with one of its ranged weapons as if it were your Shooting phase, or make one attack with one of its melee weapons as if it were the Fight phase. After resolving these attacks, the destroyed model is then removed.

ARCANA MECHANICUM: THE EYE OF XI-LEXUM

Xi-Lexum was a legend of Agripinaa. A servo-skull has been made from the cranium of the fallen Tech-Priest, so that even in death his withering gaze can reveal the weaknesses of every foe.

Agripinaa model only. At the start of your Shooting phase, select one enemy **Vehicle** unit within 18" of the bearer. Until the end of the phase, the bearer gains the following ability:

'The Eye of Xi-Lexum (Aura): While a friendly **Agripinaa Core** or **Agripinaa Kataphron Servitors** unit is within 6" of this model, each time a model in that unit makes an attack that targets the selected **Vehicle** unit, you can re-roll the wound roll.'

INDENTURED MACHINES   1CP

Agripinaa – Requisition Stratagem

With influxes of fresh converts, Agripinaa can select specimens capable of bonding to more powerful servitor enhancements.

Use this Stratagem before the battle. Select one **Agripinaa Kataphron Servitors** unit from your army. Add 1 to the Toughness characteristic of models in that unit. A unit can only be selected for this Stratagem once. You can only use this Stratagem once, unless you are playing a Strike Force battle (in which case you can use this Stratagem twice), or an Onslaught battle (in which case you can use this Stratagem three times).

THE ICON OF AGRIPINAA SHOWS THE SACRED COG AND A HERMETIC SYMBOL, WHICH SOME TECH-PRIESTS BELIEVED TO BE A REPRESENTATION OF THE CADIAN GATE.

FORGE WORLDS

GRAIA

The coldly logical forces of Graia pursue their goals no matter the cost. They believe victory to be an irrefutable certainty, subject to the ineffable wisdom of the Machine God, whose technological miracles are the only unexplainable phenomena they accept.

DOGMA: REFUSAL TO YIELD

The cortexes of those who serve Graia are so hardwired to pure logic that the most esoteric attacks break down before a wall of sheer rationality.

- Each time a Combat Attrition test is taken for a unit with this dogma, it is automatically passed.
- Each time a model with this dogma would lose a wound as a result of a mortal wound, roll one D6: on a 5+, that wound is not lost.

WARLORD TRAIT: MANTRA OF DISCIPLINE

Dogmatic imperatives rigidly enforce the duty of all who bear Graia's holy icon, the Tech-Priests' directives obeyed automatically and instantaneously.

In your opponent's Charge phase, at the start of the Heroic Interventions step, select one friendly **Graia Core** unit within 9" of this **Warlord**. Until the end of the phase:

- If that unit is within 6" horizontally and 5" vertically of any enemy unit, it is eligible to perform Heroic Interventions as if it were a **Character** unit.
- Each time a model in that unit makes a Heroic Intervention move, it can move up to 6".

ARCANA MECHANICUM: THE CEREBRAL TECHNO-MITRE

Perhaps the most famous of all cogitator engines is the Cerebral Techno-Mitre, a secondary brain that uses synaptic links to directly assist the bearer's own mental capacities. Even amidst the maelstrom of battle, the device runs complex algorithms to suggest the best course of action.

Graia Tech-Priest model only. Add 3" to the range of the bearer's aura abilities (to a maximum of 9"). Each time the bearer uses an ability in your Command phase that specifies a range, you can add 3" to the range of that ability (to a maximum of 9").

STEEL MIND, IRON LOGIC	1CP

Graia – Wargear Stratagem

Even the vile energy surges of the warp will be quieted by the faith and undeniable logic that emanates from the pure devotees of Graia.

Use this Stratagem in your opponent's Psychic phase, when an enemy **Psyker** attempts to manifest a psychic power within 18" of any **Graia** units from your army. Roll one D6: on a 4+, that psychic power is denied.

THE RISING SUN AT THE HEART OF GRAIA'S ICON SIGNIFIES THE DAWN OF A NEW AGE, WHILE THE SURROUNDING COG SHOWS THE TECH-PRIESTS TO BE ITS MASTERS.

STYGIES VIII

The Tech-Priests of Stygies VIII are trusted by few other forge worlds, their deeds and motivations occluded from their peers. Their wary caution shields their works from their enemies and allies alike.

DOGMA: SHROUD PROTOCOLS

When the armies of Stygies VIII march to war, they do so beneath stealth-screen projectors and target-befouling apparatuses.

- Each time a ranged attack targets a **Vehicle** unit (excluding units with the **Core** keyword) with this dogma, if the attacker is more than 18" away, then the target is treated as having the benefits of Dense Cover against that attack (see the Warhammer 40,000 Core Book).
- Each time a ranged attack targets a unit (excluding **Vehicle** units without the **Core** keyword) with this dogma, if the attacker is more than 12" away, then the target is treated as having the benefits of Dense Cover against that attack.
- Each time a unit with this dogma declares a charge, none of the targets of that charge can Hold Steady or Set to Defend.

WARLORD TRAIT: VEILED HUNTER

In silent supplication, a concentrated burst of noospheric negation manifests as a heavy band of shadow, directing the warriors of Stygies to obfuscate the foe's sensors and confuse their strategy.

At the start of the first battle round, you can select up to two friendly **Stygies VIII** units wholly within your deployment zone. Remove those units from the battlefield, then set them up anywhere on the battlefield that is wholly within your deployment zone. If the mission uses the Strategic Reserves rules, any of those units can be placed into Strategic Reserves without having to spend any additional CPs, regardless of how many units are already in Strategic Reserves. If both players have abilities that redeploy units, roll off; the winner chooses who redeploys their units first.

ARCANA MECHANICUM: THE OMNISSIAH'S HAND

The Omnissiah's Hand is a gauntlet lined with a concealed array of digital lasers, believed to be of Jokaero origin. Many a Tech-Adept of Stygies VIII has tried to replicate its technology, thus far to no avail.

Stygies VIII model only. Once per battle, at the end of the Fight phase, you can use this Relic. If you do so, roll one D6 for each enemy unit within 12" of the bearer: on a 2-5, that enemy unit suffers 1 mortal wound; on a 6, that enemy unit suffers D3 mortal wounds.

CLANDESTINE INFILTRATION   1CP

Stygies VIII – Wargear Stratagem

Under cover of stealth screens and auspex scramblers, the warriors of Stygies VIII confound their foes.

Use this Stratagem during deployment. Select one **Stygies VIII Core Infantry** unit from your army. When you set up that unit, it can be set up anywhere on the battlefield that is more than 9" away from the enemy deployment zone and any enemy models.

THE ICON OF STYGIES VIII SYMBOLISES NOT JUST ENLIGHTENMENT, BUT THE ACQUISITION OF KNOWLEDGE NO MATTER HOW STEEP THE COST.

FORGE WORLDS

RYZA

Ryza is famous for its mastery of advanced technologies lost to some other forge worlds. Beset on all sides, its Tech-Priests do not hesitate to unleash every arcane device and esoteric relic upon their enemies, and relish witnessing the holy effects up close.

DOGMA: RED IN COG AND CLAW

Ryza's masters point to aggressive combat doctrines and zealous training protocols to explain the exceptional martial prowess of their troops, their apparent eagerness to shed blood merely a by-product of holy fervour.

- Each time a model with this dogma makes a melee attack, if it made a charge move, was charged, or performed a Heroic Intervention this turn, add 1 to that attack's wound roll.
- Add 1 to charge rolls made for units with this dogma.

WARLORD TRAIT: CITATION IN SAVAGERY

With binharic exultations, the Tech-Priest accompanies the rending blows of Ryza's troops in a cybernetic chorus that venerates the Machine God and infuses the warriors with zealous savagery.

At the start of the Fight phase, select one friendly **Ryza Core** unit within 6" of this **Warlord**. Until the start of the next Fight phase, each time a model in that unit makes a melee attack, the Armour Penetration characteristic of that attack is improved by 1.

ARCANA MECHANICUM: WEAPON XCIX

Ryza is the rare forge world that believes in innovation, and their top Tech-Priests all have their own experimental weapons under development. Such devices often never reach the battlefield, but the up-volted volkite blaster known only as Weapon XCIX has proved its incredible prowess in battle on numerous occasions.

Ryza model equipped with a volkite blaster only. This Relic replaces a volkite blaster and has the following profile:

WEAPON	RANGE	TYPE	S	AP	D
Weapon XCIX	24"	Heavy 3	7	-2	2

Abilities: Each time an attack is made with this weapon, on an unmodified wound roll of 6, that attack inflicts 2 mortal wounds in addition to any normal damage.

PLASMA SPECIALISTS   2CP

Ryza – Battle Tactic Stratagem

That which hates most breeds the most incandescent of blasts – or so say the Tech-Priests of Ryza, who have long nurtured the secret skill of coaxing extra firepower from plasma weapons.

Use this Stratagem in your Shooting phase, when a **Ryza** unit is selected to shoot. Until the end of the phase, each time a model in that unit makes an attack with a plasma weapon (pg 112), add 1 to the Damage characteristic of that attack.

THE ILLUMINATED 'R' OF RYZA'S ICON INCORPORATES THE SKULL AND COG OF MARS, A NOD TOWARDS RYZA'S ANCESTRY.

METALICA

The zealots of Metalica purge unholy sites and cleanse the disorderly from the Machine God's realm with excoriating fervour.

DOGMA: RELENTLESS MARCH

Those of Metalica relentlessly obliterate their foes to a deafening clamour redolent of the forge world's endless industry.

- Models with this dogma do not suffer the penalty to hit rolls incurred for firing Assault weapons in the same turn that their unit has Advanced.
- Models with this dogma do not suffer the penalty to hit rolls incurred for firing Heavy weapons in the same turn that their unit has moved.
- While an enemy unit is within Engagement Range of a unit from your army with this dogma, that enemy unit is treated as being at below Half-strength.

WARLORD TRAIT: TRIBUTE OF EMPHATIC VENERATION

A cacophonous chorale emanates from Metalica's most faithful, venerating the Omnissiah with disconcerting frequencies.

At the end of your Movement phase, select one enemy unit within 12" of this **WARLORD**. Until the start of your next Command phase, each time a model in that unit makes an attack, subtract 1 from that attack's hit roll.

ARCANA MECHANICUM: THE ADAMANTINE ARM

Powered by batteries of micro servo-engines, this entire arm has been sheathed in nigh on impenetrable adamantine, making an appendage that is mightier than any other yet invented.

METALICA model only. The bearer is equipped with this Relic in addition to their other weapons. It has the following profile:

WEAPON	RANGE	TYPE	S	AP	D
The Adamantine Arm	Melee	Melee	x3	-3	4

Abilities: Each time the bearer fights, no more than one attack can be made with this weapon. Each time an attack is made with this weapon, add 1 to that attack's hit roll.

DEAFENING ASSAULT   1CP

Metalica – Wargear Stratagem

The auditory assault of the weaponry of Metalica is so intimidating that it causes entire armies to quail, before fleeing the oncoming Adeptus Mechanicus ranks.

Use this Stratagem in your Shooting phase, when a **METALICA** unit from your army is selected to shoot. Select one enemy unit (excluding **VEHICLE** units) within 12" of that unit. Until the start of your next turn:

- Halve the Move characteristic of models in that enemy unit.
- That enemy unit cannot fire Overwatch or Set to Defend.

THE HAMMER AND IRON FIST OF METALICA IS A REMINDER OF THE FORGE WORLD'S POWER TO UNMAKE THE CORRUPTION THEY WITNESS.

FORGE WORLDS

DISTANT WORLDS

If your chosen Forge World does not have an associated dogma on pages 50-57, you must instead create their dogma. You do this by first selecting one Primary dogma from those below, and then selecting one of that Primary's associated Secondary dogmas. These two rules make up your Forge World's dogma.

RAD-SATURATED FORGE WORLD

Whether as a result of natural phenomena, ancient internecine wars fought with apocalyptic weapons or calamitous accidents caused by lost knowledge, this forge world is heavily irradiated. When holy wars of requisition are unleashed, this planet's Tech-Priests and cybernetic maniples carry the curse of invisible excoriation with them.

PRIMARY
RADIANT DISCIPLES

Each time a ranged attack targets a **Core** unit with this dogma, if the attacker is more than 12" away, subtract 1 from the Strength characteristic of that attack.

SECONDARY
LUMINARY SUFFUSION

Replace the Rad-saturation ability of models with this dogma with the following ability:

'**Extreme Rad-saturation (Aura):** While an enemy unit (excluding **Vehicle** units) is within 3" of this unit, subtract 1 from the Strength and Toughness characteristics of models in that enemy unit.'

SECONDARY
SCARIFYING WEAPONRY

Add 1 to the Strength characteristic and improve the Armour Penetration characteristic by 1 of radium weapons (pg 112) models with this dogma are equipped with.

SECONDARY
MACHINE GOD'S CHOSEN

Each time a Combat Attrition test is taken for this unit, ignore any or all modifiers.

EXPANSIONIST FORGE WORLD

The Tech-Priests of this forge world are not content to labour in isolation. They are fiercely aggressive, funding large numbers of Explorator fleets in their quest to uncover the hidden truths left by the Machine God. Always on the move, their armies are swift and manoeuvrable.

PRIMARY
ACCELERATED ACTUATORS

Each time a unit with this dogma fights, if it made a charge move, was charged or performed a Heroic Intervention this turn, then until that fight is resolved, the Armour Penetration characteristic of melee weapons models in that unit are equipped with is improved by 1.

SECONDARY
FORWARD OPERATIONS

At the start of the first battle round, each **Skitarii Core** model in your army with this dogma can make a Normal Move of up to 3". This is in addition to any other abilities they may have that allow them to make a Normal Move. They cannot end this move within 9" of any enemy models.

SECONDARY
ACQUISITIVE REACH

Add 6" to the Range characteristic of rifle and carbine weapons (pg 112) that models with this dogma are equipped with.

SECONDARY
RUGGED EXPLORATORS

- Models in this unit do not suffer the penalty to hit rolls incurred for firing Heavy weapons in the same turn that their unit has moved.
- **Vehicle** models in this unit do not suffer the penalty to hit rolls incurred for firing Assault weapons in the same turn that their unit has Advanced.

DATA-HOARD FORGE WORLD

This forge world hoarded arcane knowledge until it attained mastery in hundreds of areas of technological esoterica. Through caches of STC fragments, subversive theft from other forge worlds or even treating with xenos, this forge world's masters jealously clutch insights into ore refining, duralloy formulae, crystal-flex optics, exotic energies and the mysteries of the mechanical, or so some claim.

PRIMARY
MAGNABONDED ALLOYS

Each time a **Vehicle** model with this dogma would lose a wound, roll one D6: on a 6, that wound is not lost.

SECONDARY
OMNITRAC IMPELLORS

Add 2" to the Move characteristic of **Kataphron Servitors** and **Onager Dunecrawler** models with this dogma.

SECONDARY
AUTOSAVANT SPIRITS

- At the start of your Command phase, each **Vehicle** model in your army with this dogma regains 1 lost wound.
- Models with this dogma whose characteristics can change as they suffer damage are considered to have double the number of wounds remaining for the purposes of determining what those characteristics are.

SECONDARY
SERVO-FOCUSED AUGURIES

Each time a model with this dogma makes a ranged attack with a cognis weapon (pg 112) that targets a unit within half range, you can re-roll the hit roll.

REIGNITED FORGE WORLD

However this forge world originally fell, its forges are no longer cold. The crimes of millennia past or the corrupting touch of xenos or Chaos has been deleted in a purgation regimen centuries in the process. Having delved into the quantum layers of the forge world's datasphere, those granted the honour of reconsecrating its temples have rooted out scrapcode daemons, electrogheists, alien nanophages and mutant data-echoes. The priesthood are adept at purging such threats and have been known to employ sterilised specimens on the attack, bleeding machines and weapons of the Motive Force and becalming rampant machine spirits.

PRIMARY
PURGATION PROTOCOLS

Each time a **CORE** model with this dogma makes a ranged attack, on an unmodified wound roll of 6, the Armour Penetration characteristic of that attack is improved by 1.

SECONDARY
DATA-BLEED GENERATORS

Each time an enemy model makes a melee attack against a unit with this dogma, if that enemy model made a charge move, was charged or performed a Heroic Intervention this turn, subtract 1 from that attack's hit roll.

SECONDARY
PURIFIED DATASPHERE

Add 3" to the range of the aura abilities (excluding the Rad-saturation ability) of units with this dogma (to a maximum of 9").

SECONDARY
ENGINEERED NANOPHAGES

Each time a melee attack made by a model with this dogma is allocated to a model with a Save characteristic of 3+ or better, the Armour Penetration characteristic of that attack is improved by 1.

SLAVED SYSTEMS FORGE WORLD

This forge world is closely aligned with one of the ancient forge worlds, ascribing to its particular interpretation of technological dogma.

PRIMARY
PARENT PROTOCOLS

Select one of the following Forge Worlds and use the dogma of that Forge World as listed on pages 51-57:

Agripinaa; Graia; Lucius; Mars; Metalica; Ryza; Stygies VIII. This Primary dogma does not have any associated Secondary dogmas.

If a **CHARACTER** model with this dogma gains a Warlord Trait, they can have the Forge World Warlord Trait associated with the Forge World that you selected, instead of a Warlord Trait from pages 66-67. If it does so, replace all instances of the Forge World keyword on that Warlord Trait (e.g. **LUCIUS**), if any, with the name of the Forge World that the **CHARACTER** is from.

Unless the only units with this dogma are part of an Auxiliary Support, Super-heavy Auxiliary and/ or Fortification Network Detachment, you will gain access to the Forge World Stratagem associated with the Forge World that you selected. When using such a Stratagem, replace all instances of the Forge World keyword on that Stratagem (e.g. **LUCIUS**) with the Forge World that the units with this dogma are from.

STRATAGEMS

If your army includes any **ADEPTUS MECHANICUS** Detachments (excluding Auxiliary Support, Super-heavy Auxiliary or Fortification Network Detachments), you have access to these Stratagems, and can spend CPs to use them.

ZEALOUS CONGREGATION   2CP

Adeptus Mechanicus – Battle Tactic Stratagem

The channelling of inspiring verses of zealotry allows Electro-Priests to release the pent-up energy within them.

Use this Stratagem in the Fight phase, when an **ELECTRO-PRIESTS** unit from your army is selected to fight. Until the end of the phase, each time a model in that unit makes an attack, an unmodified hit roll of 6 automatically wounds the target.

DUNESTRIDERS   1CP

Adeptus Mechanicus – Battle Tactic Stratagem

Overloading the movement protocols of a machine is a time honoured method of increasing any mechanised advance.

Use this Stratagem in your Movement phase, when an **IRONSTRIDER ENGINE** or **SERBERYS** unit from your army is selected to Advance. Until the end of the turn:

- Each time that unit Advances, do not make an Advance roll. Instead, until the end of the phase, add 6" to the Move characteristic of models in that unit.
- The Type characteristic of Heavy weapons models in that unit are equipped with is changed to Assault.
- Models in that unit do not suffer the penalty to hit rolls incurred for firing Assault weapons in the same turn that their unit has Advanced.

ASSASSIN CONSTRUCTS   1CP

Adeptus Mechanicus – Battle Tactic Stratagem

Sicarians of the kill clades are forged into perfect killing machines.

Use this Stratagem in the Fight phase, when a **SICARIAN** unit from your army is selected to fight. If that unit made a charge move, was charged or performed a Heroic Intervention this turn, then until that fight is resolved, add 1 to the Attacks characteristic of models in that unit.

ELECTROMANCER'S WRATH   1CP

Adeptus Mechanicus – Battle Tactic Stratagem

By chanting fiery psalms in praise of the Motive Force, Electro-Priests inflame the potential of their charged fields.

Use this Stratagem in your Shooting phase. Select one enemy unit (excluding **VEHICLE** units) within 12" of an **ELECTRO-PRIESTS** unit from your army. Roll one D6, subtracting 1 if the unit being rolled for has the **CHARACTER** keyword: on a 1-5, that enemy unit suffers D3 mortal wounds; on a 6, it suffers 2D3 mortal wounds.

MACHINE SUPERIORITY   1CP

Adeptus Mechanicus – Battle Tactic Stratagem

Skitarii call upon reserves of divine strength with chants of war.

Use this Stratagem in the Fight phase, when a **SKITARII** unit from your army is selected to fight. Until the end of the phase, add 1 to the Strength characteristic of models in that unit.

ELIMINATION VOLLEY   1CP

Adeptus Mechanicus – Battle Tactic Stratagem

It is possible to overcharge the augur spirits of battle servitors, homing their detection nodes in on vulnerable systems.

Use this Stratagem in your Shooting phase, when a **KATAPHRON SERVITORS** unit from your army is selected to shoot. Until the end of the phase, each time a model in that unit makes an attack that targets a unit within half range, an unmodified hit roll of 6 automatically wounds the target.

DATASPIKE   1CP

Adeptus Mechanicus – Epic Deed Stratagem

An intense micro-burst can overload any nearby machine spirit.

Use this Stratagem in the Fight phase, when an **ADEPTUS MECHANICUS TECH-PRIEST** model in your army is selected to fight. Select one enemy **VEHICLE** unit within Engagement Range of that model. Roll one D6: on a 2-5, that enemy unit suffers D3 mortal wounds; on a 6, that enemy unit suffers D3+3 mortal wounds.

BENEVOLENCE OF THE OMNISSIAH   1CP

Adeptus Mechanicus – Epic Deed Stratagem

This protective blessing moves machine spirits to defy enemy attack.

Use this Stratagem in any phase, when an **ADEPTUS MECHANICUS VEHICLE** model in your army would lose a wound as the result of a mortal wound. Until the end of the phase, each time that model would lose a wound as the result of a mortal wound, roll one D6: on a 4+, that wound is not lost.

TECH-ADEPT   1CP

Adeptus Mechanicus – Epic Deed Stratagem

Repairing war engines damaged in the crusade is a holy task.

Use this Stratagem at the start of your Command phase or at the start of your Movement phase. Select one **ADEPTUS MECHANICUS TECH-PRIEST** model in your army.

- If it is your Command phase, that model can use its Machine Focus or Awaken the Machine ability one additional time that phase.
- If it is your Movement phase, that model can use its Master of Machines ability one additional time that phase.

MACHINE SPIRIT RESURGENT   1CP

Adeptus Mechanicus – Epic Deed Stratagem

To invigorate the failing machine spirit of a damaged vehicle is a sacred task, greatly aided by certain broadcast datahymns played in the correct sequence.

Use this Stratagem in your Command phase. Select one **Adeptus Mechanicus Vehicle** model in your army. Until the start of your next Command phase, that model is considered to have its full wounds remaining for the purposes of determining what characteristics on its profile to use.

DATA-BLESSED AUTOSERMON   2CP

Adeptus Mechanicus – Epic Deed Stratagem

Struck with an infoload of revelation, truly blessed Tech-Priests will override the sacred canticles to deliver the Machine God's adaptive wisdom.

Use this Stratagem in your Command phase. Select one **Adeptus Mechanicus** unit from your army within 6" of a friendly **Tech-Priest** model and select one Canticle (pg 85) that has not yet been active for your army. Until the start of your next Command phase, that unit counts that Canticle as being active for your army in addition to the currently active one.

ARCHEOTECH SPECIALISTS   1CP

Adeptus Mechanicus – Requisition Stratagem

Within the techno-vaults there lie many mechanised wonders that can be requisitioned during times of war.

Use this Stratagem before the battle, when you are mustering your army, if your **Warlord** has the **Adeptus Mechanicus** keyword. Select one **Adeptus Mechanicus Character** model in your army and give them one Relic (this must be a Relic they can have). Each Relic in your army must be unique, and you cannot use this Stratagem to give a model two Relics. You can only use this Stratagem once, unless you are playing a Strike Force battle (in which case you can use this Stratagem twice), or an Onslaught battle (in which case you can use this Stratagem three times).

MECHANICUS LOCUM   1CP

Adeptus Mechanicus – Requisition Stratagem

Every congregation of Tech-Priests comprises masters of arcane knowledge – zealous leaders of man and machine.

Use this Stratagem before the battle, when you are mustering your army, if your **Warlord** has the **Adeptus Mechanicus** keyword. Select one **Adeptus Mechanicus Character** model in your army and determine one Warlord Trait for that model (this must be a Warlord Trait they can have); that model is only regarded as your **Warlord** for the purposes of that Warlord Trait. Each Warlord Trait in your army must be unique (if randomly generated, re-roll duplicate results), and you cannot use this Stratagem to give a model two Warlord Traits. You can only use this Stratagem once, unless you are playing a Strike Force battle (in which case you can use this Stratagem twice), or an Onslaught battle (in which case you can use this Stratagem three times).

HOST OF THE INTERMEDIARY   1CP

Adeptus Mechanicus – Requisition Stratagem

Some exceptional Skitarii are deemed worthy enough to be grafted with a portion of a Tech-Priest's persona patterning. Serving as a partial host to one so blessed by the Omnissiah, the Skitarius is seen as semi-angelic by their peers.

Use this Stratagem before the battle, when you are mustering your army, if your **Warlord** has the **Adeptus Mechanicus** keyword. Select one **Skitarii** model in your army that has the word 'Alpha' or 'Princeps' in their profile and determine one **Skitarii** Warlord Trait for that model; that model is only regarded as your **Warlord** for the purposes of that Warlord Trait. Each Warlord Trait in your army must be unique (if randomly generated, re-roll duplicate results), and you cannot use this Stratagem to give a model two Warlord Traits. You can only use this Stratagem once, unless you are playing a Strike Force battle (in which case you can use this Stratagem twice), or an Onslaught battle (in which case you can use this Stratagem three times).

ARTEFACTOTUM   1CP

Adeptus Mechanicus – Requisition Stratagem

Skitarii are mere tools to the Tech-Priests, but some have been said to be machine-touched, their untutored instincts somehow in tune with the holiest of machine spirits. Believed to be an unknowing conduit of the Machine God, they may be granted the honour of bearing a piece of techno-arcana in the hope that the Omnissiah's power flows through them to empower it.

Use this Stratagem before the battle, when you are mustering your army. Select one **Skitarii** model in your army that has the word 'Alpha' or 'Princeps' in their profile and give them one of the following Arcana Mechanicum (this must be a Relic they could have): The Cage of Varadimas; Temporcopia; The Omniscient Mask; The Skull of Elder Nikola.

Each Relic in your army must be unique, and you cannot use this Stratagem to give a model two Relics. You can only use this Stratagem once, unless you are playing a Strike Force battle (in which case, you can use this Stratagem twice) or an Onslaught battle (in which case, you can use this Stratagem three times).

BINHARIC OVERRIDE   1CP

Adeptus Mechanicus – Strategic Ploy Stratagem

Enhanced static chants can override previous commands, allowing for rapid recalibrations, but burn out doctrina wafers.

Use this Stratagem at the start of any phase. Select one **Kastelan Robot** unit from your army and one of the available protocols found on its datasheet. That protocol replaces the one that is currently active for that unit. Until the end of the game, that unit's active protocol cannot be changed. You can only use this Stratagem once.

ACQUISITION AT ANY COST   1CP

Adeptus Mechanicus – Strategic Ploy Stratagem

In their eternal quest for the acquisition of knowledge and technology, Tech-Priests require superhuman efforts from the troops under their command.

Use this Stratagem at the start of the Morale phase. Select one objective marker on the battlefield. Until the end of the phase, each time an **Adeptus Mechanicus** unit from your army takes a Morale test, if that unit is within 6" of that objective marker, it is automatically passed.

MACHINE SPIRIT'S REVENGE   1CP

Adeptus Mechanicus – Strategic Ploy Stratagem

With the right blessings, a war engine that is no longer able to serve the Machine God can enact one final triumph.

Use this Stratagem in any phase, when an **Adeptus Mechanicus Vehicle** model in your army is destroyed. Do not roll to see if that model explodes: it does so automatically.

CIRCUITOUS ASSASSINS   1CP

Adeptus Mechanicus – Strategic Ploy Stratagem

Ruststalker hunting imperatives see them swiftly and silently encircle the foe, the hum of their blades stilled.

Use this Stratagem at the end of your Movement phase. Select one **Sicarian** unit from your army that is wholly within 9" of any battlefield edge. Remove that unit from the battlefield. In the Reinforcements step of your next Movement phase, you can set that unit back up on the battlefield anywhere that is wholly within 9" of any battlefield edge and more than 9" away from any enemy models. If the battle ends and that unit is not on the battlefield, it is destroyed.

DEEPLY SUNK TALONS   1CP

Adeptus Mechanicus – Strategic Ploy Stratagem

For those caught upon the talons of hunters whose reasoning has been pared back to finely tuned instincts, escape is unlikely.

Use this Stratagem in your opponent's Movement phase, when an enemy unit (excluding **Vehicle** units) is selected to Fall Back. If that enemy unit is within Engagement Range of any **Pteraxii Sterylizor** units from your army, roll one D6: on a 2+, until the end of the phase, that enemy unit cannot Fall Back.

TACTICA OBLIQUA   2CP

Adeptus Mechanicus – Strategic Ploy Stratagem

Cogitating several steps ahead, the Serberys Raiders obey a sudden protocol change, pulling out and leaving a rash enemy exposed.

Use this Stratagem in your opponent's Charge phase, when a **Serberys Raiders** unit from your army is selected as a target of a charge. If that unit is not within Engagement Range of any enemy units, it can make a Normal Move. Until the end of the phase, that unit cannot fire Overwatch or Set to Defend. Your opponent can then select new targets for that charge.

CRUSHING WEIGHT   1CP

Adeptus Mechanicus – Strategic Ploy Stratagem

Daubed in holy oils and wreathed in pungent incense, the piston-driven walking engines of a forge world sends ton of sacred iron into the enemy at full tilt.

Use this Stratagem in your Charge phase, when an **Ironstrider Engine** or **Kastelan Robots** unit from your army finishes a charge move. Select one enemy unit within Engagement Range of that **Ironstrider Engine** or **Kastelan Robots** unit and roll one D6 for each model in that **Ironstrider Engine** or **Kastelan Robots** unit that is within Engagement Range of that enemy unit: for each 2+, that enemy unit suffers 1 mortal wound.

ELECTRO-SHOCKED   1CP

Adeptus Mechanicus – Strategic Ploy Stratagem

The truly devout can send a sudden charge of the Motive Force pulsing through their numerous augmentations, stunning nearby foes.

Use this Stratagem at the start of the Fight phase. Select one enemy unit (excluding **Vehicle** or **Monster** units) within Engagement Range of a **Cult Mechanicus Core** or **Cult Mechanicus Character** unit from your army. Until the end of the phase, that enemy unit is not eligible to fight until after all eligible units from your army have done so.

BOOSTER THRUST   1CP

Adeptus Mechanicus – Strategic Ploy Stratagem

There are none that can hide from the omniscient predation of the Machine God's devout, who soar skywards before arcing back at hunting speed.

Use this Stratagem at the end of your turn. Select one **Pteraxii** unit from your army. Remove that unit from the battlefield. In the Reinforcements step of your next Movement phase, you can set that unit back up on the battlefield anywhere that is more than 9" away from any enemy models. If the battle ends and that unit is not on the battlefield, it is destroyed.

SEISMIC BOMB   1CP

Adeptus Mechanicus – Wargear Stratagem

Blasted into the strata by powerful rockets, seismic bombs erupt in savage vibrations that throw warriors from their feet and disrupt drive units.

Use this Stratagem in your Movement phase, when an **Archaeopter Fusilave** model finishes a move. Select one enemy unit that model moved over this phase (excluding **Titanic** units or units that can **Fly**). Until the start of your next Movement phase, that enemy unit is shaken. While a unit is shaken:

- Halve the Move characteristic of models in that unit.
- Halve Advance rolls and charge rolls made for that unit.

CHAIN-TASER PROTOCOLS — 1CP

Adeptus Mechanicus – Wargear Stratagem

Accompanied by cracks of displaced air and the tang of burnt ozone, taser weapons unleash multiple forks of burning energy with every strike.

Use this Stratagem in the Fight phase, when an **ADEPTUS MECHANICUS** unit from your army is selected to fight. Until the end of the phase, each time a model in that unit makes an attack with a taser weapon (pg 112), an unmodified hit roll of 5 scores 2 additional hits.

INFOSLAVE SKULL — 2CP

Adeptus Mechanicus – Wargear Stratagem

Mono-task infoslave skulls make ideal lookouts to watch against the sudden deployment of enemy troops.

Use this Stratagem at the end of the Reinforcements step of your opponent's Movement phase. Select one **ADEPTUS MECHANICUS CORE** unit from your army that is not within Engagement Range of any enemy units. That unit can shoot as if it were your Shooting phase, but its models can only target a single eligible enemy unit that was set up as Reinforcements this turn and that is within 12" of their unit when doing so.

ELECTRO-FILAMENT COUNTERMEASURES — 2CP

Adeptus Mechanicus – Wargear Stratagem

A glittering cloud of nanofibres descends, its distorting and fracturing effect shutting down enemy comms.

Use this Stratagem at the end of your Movement phase. Select one **ARCHAEOPTER** model in your army that is equipped with a command uplink and one enemy unit within 6" of that model. Until the start of your next Movement phase, that enemy unit is not affected by the aura abilities of other enemy units.

ARC GRENADES — 1CP

Adeptus Mechanicus – Wargear Stratagem

These grenades explode with crackling power and a savage pulse of radiation that incinerates even shielded mechanical systems.

Use this Stratagem in your Shooting phase, when an **ADEPTUS MECHANICUS ARC GRENADES** unit from your army is selected to shoot. Select one enemy **VEHICLE** unit within 6" of that unit. Roll one D6: on a 2-5, that **VEHICLE** unit suffers D3 mortal wounds; on a 6, that **VEHICLE** unit suffers 2D3 mortal wounds.

INCENSE EXHAUSTS — 1CP

Adeptus Mechanicus – Wargear Stratagem

The sacred war engines of the Adeptus Mechanicus release clouds of cloying incense laced with radioactive particulate, obscuring them from enemy sensors.

Use this Stratagem in your opponent's Shooting phase, when an **ADEPTUS MECHANICUS SMOKESCREEN** unit from your army is selected as the target of an attack. Until the end of the phase, each time an attack is made against that unit, subtract 1 from that attack's hit roll.

ENRICHED ROUNDS — 1CP

Adeptus Mechanicus – Wargear Stratagem

Sanctified with the Tri-fold Litany, each of these slugs has spent a decade in the oldest and most irradiated forge temple to certify their lethality.

Use this Stratagem in your Shooting phase, when an **ADEPTUS MECHANICUS** unit from your army is selected to shoot. Until the end of the phase, each time a model in that unit makes an attack with a radium weapon (pg 112) against an enemy unit (excluding **VEHICLE** units), an unmodified hit roll of 4+ automatically wounds the target.

GALVANIC VOLLEY FIRE — 2CP

Adeptus Mechanicus – Wargear Stratagem

Experienced Rangers enter a trance-like state, their bionic augmentations working in a synchronous blur to load, fire and reload in a cycle of well-oiled automation.

Use this Stratagem in your Shooting phase, when a **SKITARII RANGERS** unit from your army is selected to shoot. Until the end of the phase, galvanic rifles models in that unit are equipped with have a Type characteristic of Rapid Fire 2.

OVERLOADED SYSTEMS — 1CP/2CP

Adeptus Mechanicus – Wargear Stratagem

Once a breach is made, the questing tendrils of the Motive Force jump from subsystem to subsystem, temporarily overloading the animus of aberrant machines.

Use this Stratagem in any phase, when an enemy **VEHICLE** model loses one or more wounds as a result of an attack made with an arc weapon (pg 112) by an **ADEPTUS MECHANICUS** model in your army. If that enemy **VEHICLE** model's characteristics can change as it suffers damage, roll one D6: on a 2+, until the start of your next Command phase, that enemy **VEHICLE** is considered to have half the number of wounds remaining for the purposes of determining what those characteristics are. If that enemy model has the **TITANIC** keyword, this Stratagem costs 2CP; otherwise it costs 1CP.

HOLY ORDERS

If your army is Battle-forged and includes any **ADEPTUS MECHANICUS** Detachments (excluding Auxiliary Support, Super-heavy Auxiliary or Fortification Network Detachments), then when you muster your army, you can induct any of the **ADEPTUS MECHANICUS TECH-PRIEST** units from your army into a Holy Order.

When you induct a **TECH-PRIEST** unit, its Power Rating is increased, as shown in the table below If you are playing a matched play game, or a game that uses a points limit, then the points value of that unit is also increased by the amount shown in the same table. Make a note on your army roster when you induct a unit into a Holy Order.

HOLY ORDER	POINTS	POWER LEVEL
Genetors	+25	+1
Logi	+35	+2
Magi	+30	+2
Artisans	+25	+1

When you induct a unit into a Holy Order it gains two additional abilities, based on which Order it is inducted into, one of which is a progressive ability (see below).

A Crusade force cannot start with any **TECH-PRIEST** units inducted into Holy Orders – to include one in a Crusade force, you must use the Holy Orders Requisition (pg 74).

You cannot induct named characters into Holy Orders using these rules. An army (and a Crusade force) cannot contain more than one **TECH-PRIEST** unit that has been inducted into each Holy Order.

PROGRESSIVE ABILITIES

Each of these abilities is made up of two separate parts – an Initial part and an Advanced part. At the start of the battle, only the Initial part is active for that model. In order for the Advanced part to become active for that model, they can perform the following action:

'**Activate Advanced Protocols (Action):** At the start of your Command phase, this model can start to perform this action. The action is completed at the start of your next Command phase. When it is completed, the Initial part of this model's progressive ability stops being active, and its Advanced part becomes active instead.'

GENETORS

Genetors probe the mysteries of the biological. Molecular striation, cyborg interfaces, genetic manipulation and alchemical behavioural modification are all avenues of interest to those determined to master the boundaries of the flesh.

When inducted into this Holy Order, the **TECH-PRIEST** model gains the following abilities:

ABILITY: ADAPTIVE MASTERY

Adaptive Mastery: Once per battle, if this model is on the battlefield when you use an Adeptus Mechanicus Battle Tactic Stratagem, reduce the CP cost of that Stratagem by 1CP. Note that the CP cost is only reduced by 1CP for that use of the Stratagem, any future usages of it cost the normal amount of CPs.

PROGRESSIVE ABILITY: LEARNINGS OF THE GENETOR

INITIAL PART

Biochemical Aggression: In your Command phase, if this part is active for this model, select one friendly **<FORGE WORLD> CORE** or **<FORGE WORLD> KATAPHRON SERVITORS** unit within 6" of this model. Until the start of your next Command phase, each time a model in that unit makes a melee attack, an unmodified hit roll of 6 automatically wounds the target.

ADVANCED PART

Hypercybernetic Physiology: In your Command phase, if this part is active for this model, select one friendly **<FORGE WORLD> KATAPHRON SERVITORS** or **<FORGE WORLD> SERVITORS** unit within 6" of this model. Until the start of your next Command phase, each time a model in that unit would lose a wound, roll one D6: on a 6, that wound is not lost.

LOGI

Data-vores and biocogitators, logi amass huge stores of information. They analyse data from thousands of sources at once until they can rationalise every move the enemy makes.

When inducted into this Holy Order, the **TECH-PRIEST** model gains the following abilities:

ABILITY: SCRIPTURAL PROGNOSIS

Scriptural Prognosis: Once per battle, if this model is on the battlefield when you use an Adeptus Mechanicus Strategic Ploy Stratagem, reduce the CP cost of that Stratagem by 1CP. Note that the CP cost is only reduced by 1CP for that use of the Stratagem, any future usages of it cost the normal amount of CPs.

PROGRESSIVE ABILITY: ANALYSES OF THE LOGOS

INITIAL PART

Predicted Barrage: In your Command phase, if this part is active for this model, select one friendly **<FORGE WORLD> CORE** unit within 6" of this model. Until the start of your next Command phase, each time an attack with an Armour Penetration characteristic of -1 or -2 is allocated to a model in that unit, that attack has an Armour Penetration characteristic of 0 instead.

ADVANCED PART

Flaws of the Foe: In your Command phase, if this part is active for this model, select one friendly **<FORGE WORLD> CORE** or **<FORGE WORLD> KATAPHRON SERVITORS** unit within 6" of this model. Until the start of your next Command phase, each time a model in that unit makes a ranged attack, the target does not receive the benefits of cover against that attack.

MAGI

Magi are masters of fiercely guarded knowledge, pursuing esoteric agendas to enhance their specialisms at all costs. No risk is too great and no gambit too unwise in their ceaseless and predatory acquisition of ancient lore.

When inducted into this Holy Order, the **TECH-PRIEST** model gains the following abilities:

ABILITY: AGGRESSIVE SUBROUTINES

Aggressive Subroutines: Once per battle, if this model is on the battlefield when you use an Adeptus Mechanicus Epic Deed Stratagem, reduce the CP cost of that Stratagem by 1CP. Note that the CP cost is only reduced by 1CP for that use of the Stratagem, any future usages of it cost the normal amount of CPs.

PROGRESSIVE ABILITY: DIVINATIONS OF THE MAGOS

INITIAL PART

Predatory Programming: In your Command phase, if this part is active for this model, select one friendly **<FORGE WORLD> CORE** unit within 6" of this model. Until the start of your next Command phase, add 2 to Advance rolls made for that unit.

ADVANCED PART

Overloaded Safeguards: In your Command phase, if this part is active for this model, select one friendly **<FORGE WORLD> CORE** unit within 6" of this model. Until the start of your next Command phase, each time a model in that unit makes a ranged attack, an unmodified hit roll of 6 scores 1 additional hit.

ARTISANS

Artisans of the Adeptus Mechanicus create wondrous artefacts of war. They install circuits of such beauty, and capacitor-nodes of such fine calibration, that their machine spirits respond with divine gratitude.

When inducted into this Holy Order, the **TECH-PRIEST** model gains the following abilities:

ABILITY: ARCHEOTECH MODIFICATIONS

Archeotech Modifications: Once per battle, if this model is on the battlefield when you use an Adeptus Mechanicus Wargear Stratagem, reduce the CP cost of that Stratagem by 1CP. Note that the CP cost is only reduced by 1CP for that use of the Stratagem, any future usages of it cost the normal amount of CPs.

PROGRESSIVE ABILITY: FABRICATIONS OF THE ARTISAN

INITIAL PART

Enhanced Biomechanical Interface: At the end of your Movement phase, if this part is active for this model, select one friendly **<FORGE WORLD> CORE** or **<FORGE WORLD> KATAPHRON SERVITORS** unit within 6" of this model. Until the start of your next Movement phase, that unit is eligible to charge and shoot in a turn in which it Fell Back, but if it does so, each time a model in that unit makes a ranged attack, subtract 1 from that attack's hit roll.

ADVANCED PART

Exquisite Calibration: In your Command phase, if this part is active for this model, select one friendly **<FORGE WORLD> CORE** unit within 6" of this model. Until the start of your next Command phase, each time a model in that unit makes a ranged attack, add 1 to the Strength characteristic of that attack.

WARLORD TRAITS

If an **ADEPTUS MECHANICUS TECH-PRIEST** model is your **WARLORD**, you can use the Tech-Priest Warlord Traits table below to determine what Warlord Trait they have. You can either roll one D6 to randomly generate one, or you can select one. If an **ADEPTUS MECHANICUS SKITARII CHARACTER** model is your Warlord, you can instead use the Skitarii Warlord Traits table opposite to determine what Warlord Trait they have in the same manner.

When you have determined a Warlord Trait for an **ADEPTUS MECHANICUS CHARACTER** model, replace all instances of the **<FORGE WORLD>** keyword in their Warlord Trait (if any) with the name of the Forge World that your model is from.

THIS WORLD BELONGS TO MANKIND. LIQUID DIAMONITE THAT RAINS FROM THE SKY AND THE SEAMS OF TRANSURANIUM. FOR US TO EXTRACT. IT IS EVIDENT IN THE WELLS OF TRANS-SULPHUR, IN THE OF THE ALMIGHTY MACHINE GOD. IT IS THERE IN THE FASCIUM DEPOSITS LEFT YOUR PETTY CLAIMS OF PRIMACY DISGUST ME XENOS. THIS WORLD BEARS THE MARK

TECH-PRIEST WARLORD TRAITS

1. EMOTIONLESS CLARITY
With a mind blissfully unsullied by the passions common to the flesh, the warlord imparts the detached logic of his priorities unto his minions. They will know the perfection of serving without the pressures of survival.

In your Command phase, select one friendly **<FORGE WORLD> CULT MECHANICUS CORE** unit within 6" of this **WARLORD**. Until the start of your next Command phase, that unit is eligible to charge in a turn in which it Fell Back.

2. MASTERWORK BIONICS
Human flesh is an anachronism, a sad legacy of a civilisation whose time has come and gone. Perfection is in crafting.

- This **WARLORD** has a 4+ invulnerable save.
- Each time an attack is allocated to this **WARLORD**, subtract 1 from the Damage characteristic of that attack (to a minimum of 1).

3. FIRST-HAND FIELD TESTING
True innovation is rare among the forge worlds, and orthodox construct testing may take centuries of study. Once the stage of field testing is reached, however, only the truly blessed of the Machine Cult are fit to bear such works of divine creation.

When you select this Warlord Trait, select one weapon this **WARLORD** is equipped with (excluding Relics). Add 1 to the Strength and Damage characteristics of that weapon.

4. NECROMECHANIC
The blessed healing of machinery is the sign of a true shepherd of the Omnissiah's flock.

Each time this **WARLORD** uses its Master of the Machines ability, the model being repaired regains up to 3 lost wounds instead of D3.

5. CARTOGRAMMATIST
From atmospheric strata to the planet's core, the Tech-Priest has inloaded every feature of this world in advance. With such knowledge, the warlord can dispatch their servants to sites of techno-religious interest with uncanny accuracy.

When you select this Warlord Trait, select one friendly **<FORGE WORLD> CULT MECHANICUS CORE** unit from your army. That unit gains the following ability:

'**Orbital Teleportarium:** During deployment, you can set up this unit in orbit instead of setting it up on the battlefield. If you do so, then in the Reinforcements step of one of your Movement phases, you can set up this unit anywhere on the battlefield that is more than 9" away from any enemy models.'

6. SUPERVISORY RADIANCE
This warlord's devout minions all feel the Tech-Priest's watchful presence as a divine radiance. Under such holy scrutiny, warriors are imbued with the precision and strength of the Machine God's chosen.

At the start of the Fight phase, select one friendly **<FORGE WORLD> CULT MECHANICUS CORE** unit within 9" of this **WARLORD**. Until the start of the next Fight phase, each time a model in that unit makes a melee attack, you can re-roll the hit roll.

SKITARII WARLORD TRAITS

1. MULTITASKING CORTEX

The warlord's cogitative capacity is several orders of magnitude greater than a common Skitarius. Sharing a fraction of this processing power, the cogni-savant enables those under their command to focus upon several tasks at once.

In your Command phase, select one friendly **<Forge World> Skitarii Core** unit within 9" of this **Warlord,** or select one friendly **<Forge World> Core Data-tether** unit on the battlefield. Until the start of your next Command phase, if that unit is performing an action, it can make ranged attacks without that action failing.

2. BATTLE-SPHERE UPLINK

Tapping into infostacks of data emanating from across the wider battle-sphere, the warlord synchronises the warriors under their command with the flows of wisdom, feeding them targeting data at a rate that borders on prophetic.

In your Command phase, select one friendly **<Forge World> Skitarii Core** unit within 9" of this **Warlord,** or select one friendly **<Forge World> Core Data-tether** unit on the battlefield. Until the start of your next Command phase, models in that unit do not suffer the penalty to hit rolls incurred for firing:

- Heavy weapons in the same turn that their unit has moved.
- Assault weapons in the same turn that their unit has Advanced.

3. PROGRAMMED RETREAT

Taking direct control of their cohorts' manoeuvres, the warlord sees their solders' withdrawal carried out with such precision that they can be immediately pressed back into efficacious service.

In your Command phase, select one friendly **<Forge World> Skitarii Core** unit within 9" of this **Warlord,** or select one friendly **<Forge World> Core Data-tether** unit on the battlefield. Until the start of your next Command phase, that unit is eligible to shoot in a turn in which it Fell Back.

4. ARCHIVED ENGAGEMENTS

Drawing upon the minutiae of servo-recorded conflicts, the warlord feeds adjusted protocols into the data-nets of their warriors, granting them a hyper-predictive combat awareness.

In your Command phase, select one friendly **<Forge World> Skitarii Core** unit within 9" of this **Warlord,** or select one friendly **<Forge World> Core Data-tether** unit on the battlefield. Until the start of your next Command phase, if that unit is within Engagement Range of any enemy units at the start of the Fight phase, it can fight first that phase.

5. FIREPOINT TELEMETRY CACHE

Optimal firepoints have been surveyed and stored by the warlord in encoded crypto-caches. When the cache seals are broken the warlord directs his charges in the golden ratios of obscuration.

In your Command phase, select one friendly **<Forge World> Skitarii Core** unit within 9" of this **Warlord,** or select one friendly **<Forge World> Core Data-tether** unit on the battlefield. Until the start of your next Command phase, each time a ranged attack is allocated to a model in that unit:

- It is treated as receiving the benefits of Light Cover against that attack (see the Warhammer 40,000 Core Book).
- If that model is entirely on or within a terrain feature and has the **Infantry** keyword, add an additional 1 to any armour saving throw made against that attack.

6. EYES OF THE OMNISSIAH

The warlord accumulates datapoints from servo-skulls in order to catalogue enemy movements, allowing their Skitarii to ambush enemies.

In your Command phase, select one friendly **<Forge World> Skitarii Core** unit within 9" of this **Warlord,** or select one friendly **<Forge World> Core Data-tether** unit on the battlefield. Until the start of your next Command phase, you can re-roll Advance rolls and charge rolls made for that unit.

RELICS

If your army is led by an **Adeptus Mechanicus Warlord**, you can, when mustering your army, give one of the following Arcana Mechanicum to an **Adeptus Mechanicus Character** model in your army. Named characters cannot be given any of the following Relics.

When a model in your army is given an Arcana Mechanicum, replace all instances of the **<Forge World>** keyword on that Relic's rules (if any) with the name of the Forge World that your model is drawn from.

Note that some Relics replace one of the model's existing items of wargear. Where this is the case, you must, if you are using points values, still pay the cost of the wargear that is being replaced. Write down any Arcana Mechanicum your models have on your army roster.

THE UNCREATOR GAUNTLET

The Uncreator Gauntlet was originally devised to reverse-engineer lost technologies. When laid upon a machine, xenotech fields are released that cause the construct's chronology to be wound back. If the timing is accurate to the picosecond, the temporal anomaly can rejuvenate the machine to the prime of its operative lifespan – or go on to reduce it to a neatly arrayed pile of component parts, each ready for the Tech-Priest's inspection.

Model equipped with a power fist only. This Relic replaces a power fist and has the following profile:

WEAPON	RANGE	TYPE	S	AP	D
The Uncreator Gauntlet	Melee	Melee	x2	-3	3

Abilities: Each time the bearer fights, it makes 1 additional attack with this weapon. Each time an attack made with this weapon hits a **Vehicle** unit, that attack inflicts 1 mortal wound in addition to any normal damage.

RAIMENT OF THE TECHNOMARTYR

This baroque suit of armour contains dozens of life-sustaining machine spirits that buzz within its fibre bundles like stinging insects. At a simple conjuration, these spirits swarm out to inhabit the weapons of those nearby. Guns that have been graced by one of these excitable animas can pour volleys of fire into the enemy, even when their wielders falter.

- Each time the bearer would lose a wound, roll one D6: on a 5+, that wound is not lost.

- In your Command phase, select one friendly **<Forge World> Core** unit within 3" of this model. Until the start of your next Command phase, each time a model in that unit makes a ranged attack, you can ignore any or all hit roll and Ballistic Skill modifiers.

THE SKULL OF ELDER NIKOLA

This yellowed, multi-lacquered servo-skull is perhaps the most ancient of its kind. It has been ghostdated to the early days of Mankind. Should the correct praise-psalm be sung to it, the halo of electrical power that surrounds the skull's bony circumference will explode outwards in a ring of crackling force, scrambling the unnatural workings of enemy war engines.

At the start of your Shooting phase, roll one D6 for each enemy **Vehicle** unit within 12" of the bearer: on a 2-3, that unit suffers 1 mortal wound; on a 4-5, that unit suffers D3 mortal wounds; on a 6, that unit suffers 3 mortal wounds.

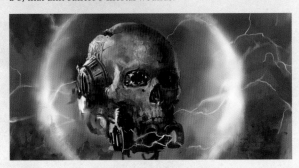

THE PURGATION'S PURITY

This serpenta's bullets contain cores of quasi-stabilised polonium. Even grazing hits have been known to overwhelm the post-human physiology of Traitor Astartes, their flesh sloughing away in black chunks in a localised rad-storm.

Model equipped with a radium serpenta only. This Relic replaces a radium serpenta and has the following profile:

WEAPON	RANGE	TYPE	S	AP	D
Purgation's Purity	24"	Assault 3	4	-2	2

Abilities: Each time an attack is made with this weapon, an unmodified hit roll of 4+ automatically wounds the target.

EXEMPLAR'S ETERNITY

Among the verbose tracts on martial dogma penned by the Secutors of Mars, the name Trantium-01 is appended in micro-scriptum to treatise after treatise. Before expiration, the venerable Marshal was hailed by Mars as a Skitarius Exemplar and – in death – was refashioned into a servo skull; a singular honour for the usually disposable Skitarii.

Skitarii Marshal model only. The bearer's Servo-skull Uplink ability is replaced with the following ability:

'**Exemplar's Eternity (Aura):** While a friendly **<Forge World> Skitarii Core** unit is within 6" of this model, each time a model in that unit makes an attack, re-roll a hit roll of 1 and re-roll a wound roll of 1.'

PHOSPHOENIX

Having seen the horror of the living, blue-white flame of phosphex weaponry, Tech-Priest Veriliad destroyed the lone STC for the substance's creation. Efforts to recreate it have been unsuccessful ever since. Decried as Heretic Technis by the rest of his order, Veriliad was tied to a stake and shot with the pistol known as Phosphoenix, the finest phosphex weapon ever produced.

Model equipped with a phosphor serpenta only. This Relic replaces a phosphor serpenta and has the following profile:

WEAPON	RANGE	TYPE	S	AP	D
Phosphoenix	18"	Assault 3	5	-3	2

Abilities: Each time an attack is made with this weapon, the target does not receive the benefits of Dense Cover against that attack. Each time an attack is made with this weapon against an enemy unit, if a hit is scored, until the end of the phase, that enemy unit is exposed and the bearer gains the following ability:

'**Target Exposure (Aura):** While a friendly **<Forge World> Core** unit is within 6" of this model, each time a model in that unit makes a ranged attack against an exposed unit, the target does not receive the benefits of Dense Cover against that attack.'

PATER COG-TOOTH

Legends told in binharic code claim that this axe is the first of its kind. Built on Mars, the Pater Cog-Tooth is a venerable weapon that seems to glow with an aura of power, although perhaps that is simply rad-emanations dating from the Great Cataclysm of Mars.

Model equipped with an Omnissian axe only. This Relic replaces an Omnissian axe and has the following profile:

WEAPON	RANGE	TYPE	S	AP	D
Pater Cog-tooth	Melee	Melee	+3	-2	3

ANZION'S PSEUDOGENETOR

Appearing as a nest of mechadendrites, this device can be set to dissect a nearby alien organism with startling speed. Blood sprays, paralytic elixirs are administered, skin is peeled from muscle and muscle parted from endoskeleton. The wearer watches as his device files away observations upon the biomechanics of the foe, until the specimen collapses in a mess of viscera and bone.

The bearer is equipped with this Relic in addition to their other weapons. It has the following profile:

WEAPON	RANGE	TYPE	S	AP	D
Anzion's Pseudogenetor	Melee	Melee	+2	-1	1

Abilities: Each time the bearer fights, it makes 3D3 additional attacks with this weapon.

THE OMNISCIENT MASK

Legend has it that the wearer of the Omniscient Mask can read the souls of men. An object of great veneration amongst the Skitarii, those under its gaze fight all the harder.

The bearer gains the following ability:

'**The Omniscient Mask (Aura):** While a friendly **<Forge World> Skitarii Core** unit is within 6" of this model, each time a model in that unit makes a melee attack, an unmodified hit roll of 6 scores 1 additional hit.'

SONIC REAPER

Multiple reflectors, each formed of unique materials and microscopically shaped to a unique template, line the frequency emitters of this relic transonic cannon. It is reputed to be the same instrument that Rem van Diserys wrote about before his disappearance. In the remnants of his journal – that continue to vibrate in quantum states to this day – he described the painful demise of the Scurata Metroplex and their inhuman xenos screams, as their constituent molecules were shaken apart.

Model equipped with a transonic cannon only. This Relic replaces a transonic cannon and has the following profile:

WEAPON	RANGE	TYPE	S	AP	D
Sonic Reaper	12"	Assault D6	5	-2	2

Abilities: Each time an attack is made with this weapon, that attack automatically hits the target. Each time an attack is made with this weapon, an unmodified wound roll of 5-6 inflicts 2 mortal wounds on the target and the attack sequence ends.

TEMPORCOPIA

It is thought – by Mars at least – that no forge world retains the knowledge of nano-engineering, despite its horror being so prevalent during the Age of Technology. The Temporcopia is a relic from that dark time, yet its constituent, microscopic machines replicate to a given sacred number and no more. Released from their magnetic casket, the invisible devices seek out nearby prey, sinking between molecular bonds and draining electro-chemical potential for a moment before they expire.

At the start of the Fight phase, you can select one enemy unit within 3" of the bearer. That unit is not eligible to fight this phase until after all eligible units from your army have done so.

THE CAGE OF VARADIMAS

The Cage of Varadimas is a single, continuous electro-circuit of ancient and exquisite design. Its implantation is excruciating until one has tamed its coruscating power. The crippling charge it emits can throw an Ork back several feet, causing nerves and muscles to twitch uncontrollably, and leaving the enemy easy prey for Tech-Priests who indulge in battlefield vivisection. All it takes is a touch and the potent change passes from one target to another.

Each time the bearer hits an enemy unit (excluding **Vehicle** units) with a melee attack, until the end of the phase, that unit is electro-shocked. Each time a model in an electro-shocked unit makes an attack, subtract 1 from that attack's hit roll.

CHAPTER APPROVED RULES

If every model in your army (excluding **Agent of the Imperium** and **Unaligned** units) has the **Adeptus Mechanicus** keyword, and your **Warlord** has the **Adeptus Mechanicus** keyword, you can, if you are playing a matched play battle that instructs you to select secondary objectives (e.g. a mission from the Eternal War mission pack in the Warhammer 40,000 Core Book), select one of them to be from the Adeptus Mechanicus secondary objectives listed below.

Like all other secondary objectives, each of the secondary objectives listed below has a category, and they follow all the normal rules for secondary objectives (for example, when you select secondary objectives, you cannot choose more than one from each category, you can score no more than 15 victory points from each secondary objective you select during the mission etc.).

PURGE THE ENEMY

ACCRETION OF KNOWLEDGE

End Game Objective

In the holy Quest for Knowledge that underpins the Adeptus Mechanicus' obsessive tendencies, the more powerful or esoteric the source of information the better. Ancient artefacts and destructive engines are zealously sought, and the enemy's greatest champions often hold secrets they would selfishly keep to themselves. It is time they learned that nothing is beyond the reach of the Machine Cult.

Score 3 victory points at the end of the battle for each destroyed enemy model that meets one or more of the following criteria:

- The model has a Warlord Trait.
- The model has a Relic.
- The model has the **Vehicle** keyword and a Wounds characteristic of 14 or more.

NO MERCY, NO RESPITE

ERADICATION OF FLESH

Progressive Objective

A glorious utopia is within your grasp – the Time of the Machine is at hand! Cast down the worthless heretics who have strayed from the Omnissiah's enlightenment. Let all feel the excoriating fire of the Motive Force, and may the sacred engines of destruction crunch over their weak bones without impediment.

Score 3 victory points at the end of the battle round if there is at least one **Adeptus Mechanicus Vehicle** unit from your army on the battlefield, and if **Adeptus Mechanicus** units from your army destroyed more enemy **Infantry** units this battle round than enemy units destroyed friendly **Vehicle** units.

BATTLEFIELD SUPREMACY

UNCHARTED SEQUENCING

Progressive Objective

This techno-religious site is criss-crossed with interconnected nodes of power, an ancient mechanism of undreamt potential waits to stir at your activation. Yet there is some arcane sequence to discover. The sacred formula is a test, surely laid down by the Machine God, and only those with the cogitative capacity and unremitting faith to succeed will be granted their deity's munificent blessings.

Before deployment, assign one objective marker to each battle round and note this down on your army roster. An objective marker cannot be assigned to more than one battle round. Score 3 victory points at the end of the battle round if you control the objective marker assigned to that battle round.

HIDDEN ARCHEOVAULT

Progressive Objective

Divinatory auguries have revealed the location of a vast store of technological arcana in this area, perhaps even containing a fully functioning STC database. It must be seized before the enemy has the chance to acquire or destroy it. The hidden archeovault must be held against all opposition, while reverent data-probes gradually extract fragments about its true nature.

Before deployment, your opponent selects one objective marker on the battlefield (excluding objective markers in their own deployment zone).

- Score 2 victory points at the end of the battle round if you control that objective marker.
- Score 5 victory points at the end of the battle if you control that objective marker.

CRUSADE RULES

In this section you'll find additional rules for playing Crusade battles with Adeptus Mechanicus, such as Agendas, Battle Traits and Crusade Relics that are bespoke to ADEPTUS MECHANICUS units. You can find out more about Crusade armies in the Warhammer 40,000 Core Book.

This section contains the following additional rules:

AGENDAS

ADEPTUS MECHANICUS units attempt to achieve unique Agendas in Crusade battles, which can be found on the page opposite. These Agendas represent the unique goals of Adeptus Mechanicus armies and their particular methods of waging war. You can find out more about Agendas in the Crusade mission packs, such as that presented in the Warhammer 40,000 Core Book.

REQUISITIONS

Adeptus Mechanicus armies have access to a number of additional Requisitions, suited to the individual character of their cyborg legion.

BATTLE TRAITS

ADEPTUS MECHANICUS units can be given one of the Battle Traits presented on page 75 as they gain experience and are promoted in your Crusade force. These help to reflect the unique upgrades and Battle Honours that ADEPTUS MECHANICUS units can gain.

CRUSADE RELICS

In addition to the Crusade Relics presented in the Warhammer 40,000 Core Book, Adeptus Mechanicus characters can claim one of the Crusade Relics described on page 76; these Relics are unique to the Adeptus Mechanicus, and grant the bearer power and prestige.

WEAPON ENHANCEMENTS

ADEPTUS MECHANICUS units can be equipped with one of the Weapon Enhancements presented on page 77 as they are upgraded in your Crusade force. These help to represent the deadly power of Adeptus Mechanicus weaponry on the battlefield.

ARCHEOTECH TREASURES

The Tech-Priests of the Adeptus Mechanicus are ever searching for obscure and precious pieces of technology from which they can fashion weapons of sheer destruction and objects of pure power. Pages 78-81 provide the means for your Crusade Force to build up a mighty vault of such deadly weaponry.

SHOWCASE CRUSADE ARMY

On pages 82-83 you will find Joel Martin's superb Adeptus Mechanicus Crusade army, with a description of the force and its upgrades, and details of its exploits on the battlefield.

In the ancient, abandoned undercities that form the foundations of Hive Zolara, Xixos-117 directs his attendant Skitarii to the eradication of xenos abominations. He can sense a source of power near at hand, and no mutant strain will stand before the might of Mars and its rightful acquisitions.

AGENDAS

If your Crusade army includes any **ADEPTUS MECHANICUS** units, you can select one Agenda from the Adeptus Mechanicus Agendas, listed below. This is a new category of Agendas, and follows all the normal rules for Agendas (for example, when you select Agendas, you cannot choose more than one from each category).

TECH SCAVENGERS

Adeptus Mechanicus Agenda

The greater the enemy's mechanical giants, the greater their misuse of the Omnissiah's gifts. The monstrosity must be purged in order to discover its secrets. Where there was once purity, the spark of life can yet be returned. Where there was only corruption, no part can be allowed to survive.

If you selected this Agenda, then after both sides have finished deploying, select one enemy **VEHICLE** unit with the highest Power Rating in your opponent's army. If that unit is destroyed by an **ADEPTUS MECHANICUS** unit from your army:

- That **ADEPTUS MECHANICUS** unit gains 3 experience points.
- Place a marker on the battlefield where that unit was destroyed. **ADEPTUS MECHANICUS INFANTRY** or **ADEPTUS MECHANICUS MONSTER** units from your army can attempt the following action:

'**Tech Scavenge (Action):** At the end of your Movement phase, one **ADEPTUS MECHANICUS INFANTRY** or **ADEPTUS MECHANICUS MONSTER** unit from your army that is within 3" of that marker can start to perform this action. This action is completed at the start of your next Command phase. When this action is completed, remove that marker from the battlefield and acquire one archeotech part (pg 78).'

BREAK THE SEALS

Adeptus Mechanicus Agenda

Rumour and binharic whispers have led to this place, with the promise of an unplundered archeocrypt or the buried remnants of an ancient war. For those with the fortitude to break the seals on such an ancient repository, the rewards could be great indeed.

If you selected this Agenda, then after both sides have finished deploying, randomly select one objective marker on the battlefield (excluding objective markers in your deployment zone). **ADEPTUS MECHANICUS CHARACTER** units from your army can attempt the following action:

'**Search the Vault (Action):** At the end of your Movement phase, one **ADEPTUS MECHANICUS CHARACTER** unit from your army that is within 3" of that objective marker can start to perform this action. This action is completed at the end of the turn. When this action is completed, that unit gains 1 experience point and you roll one D6: on a 5+, you acquire one archeotech weapon part (pg 80). That unit gains 1 additional experience point, and units from your army can no longer perform this action.'

OMNISSIAH'S WILL

Adeptus Mechanicus Agenda

The Omnissiah is all-seeing and all-knowing. Even in this forsaken place, those who vow to slay the unbelievers to the sonorous static-psalms demanded by doctrine may be granted divine inspiration.

If you selected this Agenda, then after both sides have finished deploying, select one Canticle of the Omnissiah (pg 85). If, while that Canticle is active for your army, three of more enemy units are destroyed by **CULT MECHANICUS** units from your army:

- Each **TECH-PRIEST** unit from your army on the battlefield gains 1 experience point.
- Each **CULT MECHANICUS** unit from your army that destroyed any enemy units while that Canticle was active for your army gains 1 experience point.

COLD LOGIC

Adeptus Mechanicus Agenda

Efficiency and the rigid application of cause and effect are valued highly by the Tech-Priests – few other metrics of success are relevant.

Keep a Domination tally for each **SKITARII** unit from your army.

- Each time an enemy unit is destroyed by a ranged attack made by a **SKITARII** model in your army, if the Protector Imperative is active for your army, add 1 to the Domination tally of that model's unit.
- Each time an enemy unit is destroyed by a melee attack made by a **SKITARII** model in your army, if the Conquerer Imperative is active for your army, add 1 to the Domination tally of that model's unit.
- At the end of your opponent's turn, if the Aggressor Imperative is active for your army, add 1 to the Domination tally of each **SKITARII** unit from your army that is within the opponent's deployment zone.
- At the end of your opponent's turn, if the Bulwark Imperative is active for your army, add 1 to the Domination tally of each **SKITARII** unit from your army that is controlling an objective marker.

At the end of the battle, the three units from your army with the highest Domination tally each gain 1 experience point.

REQUISITIONS

If your Crusade force includes any **ADEPTUS MECHANICUS** units, you can spend Requisition points (RPs) on any of the following Requisitions in addition to those presented in the Warhammer 40,000 Core Book.

ASSEMBLE ARCHEOTECH   1RP

The process of mechanical creation is a holy act undertaken with choirs of droning servitors, scores of chanting priests, sacred oils poured from bronze ewers, candles made from the bilge grime of revered ships and finally the Canticle of Humble Obeisance broadcast in Novabyte before a cell of the Motive Force is presented. Such, at least, is the process in one forge temple among thousands.

Purchase this Requisition at any time, if your Crusade force has at least one archeotech power source and one other type of archeotech. Select one power source and one other part type that you have acquired and assemble them into a new piece of archeotech, as described on pg 78-81.

Update your Order of Battle accordingly.

BODY DONOR   1RP

Influential Tech-Priests maintain subsidiary bionic bodies, onto which they transplant the remaining meat of themselves should they suffer severe damage.

Purchase this Requisition at any time when a **TECH-PRIEST** model from your Crusade Force gains a rank. Remove that model from your Order of Battle and replace it with another **TECH-PRIEST** model from the same Forge World (excluding named characters). You cannot purchase this Requisition if doing so would cause your total Power Level to exceed your Crusade force's Supply Limit. The newly added **TECH-PRIEST** model starts with the same number of experience points as the one it replaced, has the same Battle Honours, the same pieces of archeotech and is inducted into the same Holy Order, but has no Battle Scars.

UNORTHODOX ACQUISITION   3RP/5RP

There are many avenues of procurement for a wilful Tech-Priest.

Purchase this Requisition at any time. Select one type of archeotech and then either select one of that type's parts or roll one D6 to randomly determine one of that type's parts: you acquire that archeotech part and update your Order of Battle accordingly. If you rolled to determine the archeotech part, this Requisition costs 3RP; otherwise, it costs 5RP.

HOLY ORDERS   1RP

For those with the influence, induction into a Holy Order can bring patronage and power.

Purchase this Requisition when you add a **TECH-PRIEST** unit to your Order of Battle (excluding named characters), or when a **TECH-PRIEST** model in your Crusade force gains a rank. That model is inducted into one of the Holy Orders (pg 64-65); increase its Power Rating accordingly and make a note on its Crusade card. A model can never be inducted into more than one Holy Order. You cannot purchase this Requisition if doing so would cause your total Power Level to exceed your Crusade force's Supply Limit.

CONSECRATED UPGRADE   1RP/2RP

Many Tech-Priests will apply their specialist skills the right price.

Purchase this Requisition when a **SKITARII** unit (excluding **VEHICLE** units) from your army that does not contain any models with Weapon Enhancements gains one of the Weapon Enhancements found on page 77.

- If that unit has a Power Rating of 9 or less, you can remove one archeotech power source and one other archeotech part from your Order of Battle to give every model in that unit that Weapon Enhancement. That unit's Crusade points are increased by 3 and this Requisition costs 1RP.
- If that unit has a power rating of 10 or more, you can remove two archeotech power sources and two other archeotech parts from your Order of Battle to give every model in that unit that Weapon Enhancement. That unit's Crusade points are increased by 5 and this Requisition costs 2RP.

After purchasing this Requisition, models in that unit can no longer be given any further Weapon Enhancements.

'I require these cobalt interface compositors, Skand. That infuriating Trader demands them for… a consignment of promethium of sufficient quality to satisfy my Dominus. He hides behind his Warrant of Trade and the guns of his convoy, but in truth he believes his family, his,' Enginseer Rhogen-S8 gave the binharic equivalent of spitting the next word, 'genetics, place him out of Mars' reach. Surely you can perceive the logic in advancing our negotiations?'
    'You have impressed upon me at length, Enginseer: the necessity of paying this rogue's price, of obtaining his promised – promethium? – and the urgency of your master's mission.

There are procedures in this sub-sector, and I have requisitions to fill.'
    'Skand, this need not be raised with my Dominus. This delay need not even reach the cognisance of Mars. If we could…'
    'Let me intercept such a dangerous process of logic, Enginseer. This forge moon is within Holy Mars' realm, but we are a long way from the Red Planet. They would understand, I am sure, the practicalities of life out here. There are pirates that haunt this region, and the likes of your Trader friend. There are even brothers of the Cog that would sabotage your ship. Tell me about this "promethium" you want to trade for, tell me what your Dominus seeks, and perhaps your quest will succeed.'

BATTLE TRAITS

When an **ADEPTUS MECHANICUS** unit gains a Battle Trait, you can use one of the tables below instead of one of the tables in the Warhammer 40,000 Core Book to determine what Battle Trait the unit has gained. To do so, roll one D6 and consult the appropriate table to randomly determine what Battle Trait the unit gains, or choose a Battle Trait that tells the best narrative for your unit. All the normal rules for Battle Traits apply (e.g. a unit cannot have the same Battle Trait more than once). As with any Battle Honour, make a note on the unit's Crusade card when it gains a Battle Trait and increase its Crusade points accordingly, as described in the Warhammer 40,000 Core Book.

TECH-PRIEST UNITS

D6	TRAIT
1	**Machine Savant:** If this model is part of your Crusade army, and if it was not destroyed during the battle, then at the end of the battle you can ignore one failed Out of Action test taken for a **<FORGE WORLD> VEHICLE** unit – that test is treated as having been passed instead.
2	**Voltagheist Shock:** At the end of the Fight phase, select one enemy unit within Engagement Range of this model and roll one D6: on a 2-5, that unit suffers 1 mortal wound; on a 6, that unit suffers D3 mortal wounds.
3	**Repair Protocols:** Each time this model would lose a wound, roll one D6: on a 5+, that wound is not lost.
4	**Control Cortex:** You can determine one Skitarii Warlord Trait (pg 67) for this model. This model is only regarded as your **WARLORD** for the purposes of that Warlord Trait, unless it is also selected as your **WARLORD**. Each Warlord Trait in your army must be unique (if randomly generated, re-roll duplicate results), and this model cannot have more than one Warlord Trait.
5	**System-Slave Trephination:** In your Command phase, select one enemy **VEHICLE** model within 9" of this model. Then, roll one D6, adding 2 if this model's Leadership characteristic is higher than that enemy model's: on a 4+, select one weapon that enemy model is equipped with. Until the start of your next Command phase, each time that model makes an attack with that weapon, subtract 1 from that attack's hit roll.
6	**Teleportation Node:** Once per battle, at the start of your Movement phase, you can remove this model from the battlefield and then, in the Reinforcements step of your next Movement phase, you can set it back up on the battlefield, anywhere wholly within your own deployment zone and more than 9" from any enemy models. If the battle ends and this model is not on the battlefield, it is destroyed.

SKITARII MARSHAL UNITS

D6	TRAIT
1-2	**Integrated Refraction Emitters:** This model has a 4+ invulnerable save.
3-4	**Battlefield Processing Cortex:** In your Command phase, select one friendly **<FORGE WORLD> SKITARII CORE** unit within 9" of this model, or select one friendly **<FORGE WORLD> CORE DATA-TETHER** unit on the battlefield. Until the start of your next Command phase, that unit is eligible to perform Heroic Interventions as if it were a **CHARACTER**.
5-6	**Secutor Class Blade Implants:** When this model finishes a charge move, select one enemy unit within Engagement Range of it and roll one D6: on a 3-5, that unit suffers 1 mortal wound; on a 6, that unit suffers D3 mortal wounds.

CORE AND KATAPHRON SERVITORS UNITS

D6	TRAIT
1-2	**Enhance Bionics:** Improve this unit's invulnerable save by 1 (this ability cannot make this unit's invulnerable save better than 4+).
3-4	**Killcode Gear Switches:** Add 1 to the Strength characteristic of models in this unit.
5-6	**Blessed Bodies:** Each time an attack is made against this unit, an unmodified wound roll of 1-2 always fails, irrespective of any abilities that the weapon or the attacker may have.

VEHICLE UNITS

D6	TRAIT
1-2	**Sanctified Engine:** Each time this unit Advances, do not make an Advance roll. Instead, until the end of the phase, add 6" to the Move characteristic of models in this unit.
3-4	**Hardened Machine Spirit:** Out of Action tests taken for this unit are automatically passed.
5-6	**Blessed Spirit:** Each time a model in this unit would lose a wound, roll one D6: on a 6, that wound is not lost.

CRUSADE RELICS

When an **Adeptus Mechanicus Character** model gains a Crusade Relic, you can instead select one of the Relics listed below. All the usual rules for selecting Crusade Relics, as described in the Warhammer 40,000 Core Book, apply.

ARTIFICER RELICS

An **Adeptus Mechanicus Character** model can be given one of the following Artificer Relics instead of one of the ones presented in the Warhammer 40,000 Core Book.

Multiplexed Neural Inducer

Plugged into the devotee's brain matter, additional cogitation engines allow for a measure of mental control over nearby servants.

The bearer gains the following ability:

'**Multiplexed Neural Inducer (Aura):** While a friendly **<Forge World> Core** unit is within 6" of this model, that unit it is eligible to perform a Heroic Intervention as if it were a **Character**.'

Kardiocore Galvanus

Embedded in the zealot's chest cavity, this fist-sized galvanic cell pulses with rhythmic power, radiating its pounding vitality.

The bearer gains the following ability:

'**Kardiocore Galvanus (Aura):** While a friendly **<Forge World> Skitarii Core** unit is within 6" of this model, add 1 to Advance and charge rolls made for that unit.'

ANTIQUITY RELICS

An **Adeptus Mechanicus Character** model of Heroic rank or higher can be given the following Antiquity Relic instead of one of the ones presented in the Warhammer 40,000 Core Book. Add 1 to a unit's total Crusade points for each Antiquity Relic it has – this is in addition to the +1 from gaining a Battle Honour, for a total of +2.

Transinduction Body

Surreptitious theories surround this chunk of archeotech. When bolted into one's bionic body, the bearer can will their form to discorporate, allowing them to walk through solid rock.

- Each time the bearer makes a Normal Move, Advances, Falls Back or makes a charge move, until that move is finished, it can move horizontally through models and terrain features (it cannot finish a move on top of another model, or its base).
- The bearer is eligible to shoot and charge in a turn in which it Fell Back.
- The bearer can declare a charge in a turn in which it Advanced.

LEGENDARY RELICS

An **Adeptus Mechanicus Character** model of Legendary rank can be given the following Legendary Relic instead of one of the ones presented in the Warhammer 40,000 Core Book. In addition, in order to give a model a Legendary Relic, you must also pay 1 Requisition point (if you do not have enough Requisition points, you cannot give that model a Legendary Relic). Add an additional 2 to a unit's total Crusade points for each Legendary Relic it has – this is in addition to the +1 from

gaining a Battle Honour, for a total of +3.

Autocaduceus of Arkhan Land

This rod's runic tip can impart blessed energy to anything metallic that the wielder strikes. Cyborgs and engines so struck will stitch themselves back together, as if repaired by the Technoarcheologist.

Once per battle, when another friendly **<Forge World>** model within 6" of the bearer is destroyed, you can choose to roll one D6 at the end of the phase instead of using any rules that are triggered when a model is destroyed (e.g. Explodes). If you do so, then on a 3+, set that model back up on the battlefield as close as possible to where they were destroyed, and not within Engagement Range of any enemy models, with 6 wounds remaining (this cannot allow a model to have more wounds remaining than its Wounds characteristic).

On the fringes of Imperial space, an Explorator fleet's advance guard encounter the T'au. The planet's bedrock and the aliens' habitats bear the scars of orbital bombardment, and now the holy soldiery of the Skitarii have arrived to complete the purge.

WEAPON ENHANCEMENTS

When an **Adeptus Mechanicus** unit gains a Weapon Enhancement, you can, if the weapon selected is one of the weapon types listed on page 112, use the associated table below or opposite, instead of one of the tables in the Warhammer 40,000 Core Book. Once you have selected the weapon, roll one D6 and consult the appropriate table to randomly determine what Weapon Enhancement is gained, or choose the one that tells the best narrative for your unit. If the weapon you have selected is equipped on an **Infantry** or **Cavalry** model, you can instead roll two D6 (re-rolling duplicate results) or choose two. All the normal rules for Weapon Enhancements still apply. As with any Battle Honour, make a note on the unit's Crusade card when it gains a Weapon Enhancement and increase its Crusade points accordingly, as described in the Warhammer 40,000 Core Book.

ARC WEAPONS

D6	TRAIT
1-3	**Resonant Frequency:** Each time an attack is made with this weapon against a **Vehicle** unit, an unmodified wound roll of 3+ successfully wounds the target
4-6	**Shocking Overload:** After the bearer's unit has shot, select one enemy **Vehicle** model that lost one or more wounds as a result of an attack made by a model in the bearer's unit with this Weapon Enhancement. Until the start of your next Command phase, that unit is shocked. While a unit is shocked, it cannot Fall Back.

RADIUM WEAPONS

D6	TRAIT
1-3	**Thorium Rounds:** In your Shooting phase, when the bearer's unit is selected to shoot, unless the Stratagem has already been used this phase, you can use the Enriched Rounds Stratagem for 0CP. If you do so, only models with this Weapon Enhancement benefit from that Stratagem.
4-6	**Rad-sickness:** After the bearer's unit has shot, select one enemy unit that had one or more models destroyed as a result of an attack made by a model in the bearer's unit with this Weapon Enhancement. Until the start of your next Command phase, that unit is rad-sick. While a unit is rad-sick, subtract 1 from the Strength and Toughness characteristics of models in that unit. That unit is not affected by the Rad-saturation and Extreme Rad-saturation abilities.

COGNIS WEAPONS

D6	TRAIT
1-3	**Hunter Machine Spirit:** Each time an attack is made with this weapon, you can re-roll the wound roll.
4-6	**Vindictive Machine Spirit:** Each time an attack is made with this weapon that targets a unit within 12", add 1 to the Strength characteristic of that attack and improve its Armour Penetration characteristic by 1.

PLASMA WEAPONS

D6	TRAIT
1-3	**Vent Shielding:** Each time an unmodified hit roll of 1 is made with this weapon, the bearer does not suffer any mortal wounds and is not destroyed.
4-6	**Fully Charged:** Each time an attack made with this weapon targets a unit within 12", if the bearer Remained Stationary during its previous Movement phase, it makes 1 additional attack with this weapon.

PHOSPHOR WEAPONS

D6	TRAIT
1-3	**Incandescent Tracer Fire:** Each time an attack is made with this weapon that targets a unit within half range, you can re-roll the hit roll.
4-6	**Luminagen:** After the bearer's unit has shot, select one enemy unit that had one or more models destroyed as a result of an attack made by a model in the bearer's unit with this weapon attachment. Until the start of your next Command phase, that unit is on fire. While a unit is on fire, each time it makes a Normal Move, Advances or Falls Back, roll one D6 for each model in that unit: for each roll of 1, that unit suffers 1 mortal wound (to a maximum of 6 mortal wounds).

RIFLE WEAPONS

D6	TRAIT
1-3	**Phase Helix Rifling:** Add 3" to the Range characteristic of this weapon. Each time an attack is made with this weapon, if the bearer Remained Stationary during its previous Movement phase, you can ignore any or all hit roll modifiers.
4-6	**Detonation Rounds:** After the bearer's unit has shot, select one enemy unit that had one or more models destroyed as a result of an attack made by a model in the bearer's unit with this weapon attachment. Roll 2D6: if the result is equal to or less than that enemy unit's Leadership characteristic, until the end of the turn, do not roll again for that enemy unit for this ability; if the result is higher than that enemy unit's Leadership characteristic, until the start of your next Command phase, that enemy unit is suppressed. While a unit is suppressed, each time a model in that unit makes a ranged attack, that attack's hit roll and wound roll cannot be re-rolled.

CARBINE WEAPONS

D6	TRAIT
1-3	**Rapid Tracking Optics:** Each time an attack is made with this weapon, the bearer does not suffer the penalty incurred to hit rolls for firing Assault weapons in the same turn that their unit has Advanced.
4-6	**Folding Stock:** The bearer can be selected to shoot with if its unit is within Engagement Range of any enemy units and can make attacks with this weapon when doing so. If it does so, each time an attack is made with this weapon, subtract 1 from that attack's hit roll.

ARCHEOTECH TREASURES

If your Crusade Army includes any **ADEPTUS MECHANICUS** units, you can collect parts of obscure archeotech and combine them together to create unique items of incredible power.

You can gain archeotech parts by choosing and completing the relevant Agendas (pg 73) in your battles, or by using the Unorthodox Acquisition Requisition (pg 74). Keep an additional note of any archeotech parts your army has collected (the Crusade Goals, Notes and Additional Information box on your Order of Battle is ideal for this).

Archeotech Parts

When your army acquires an archeotech part, roll one D6 and consult the table below to see which type of part was found, then roll one D6 and consult the relevant table on the following pages to determine which instance of that part was found.

D6	ARCHEOTECH PART TYPE
1-3	**Power Source:** Archeotech Treasures require power sources to drive them. A power source can be combined with any of the other archeotech parts to create a final, complete item.
4	**Weapon Part:** Some of the deadliest and most arcane weapons used during the Dark Age of Technology have survived, their capabilities undimmed.
5	**Force Field Part:** Emitting pulses of energy that repel or feed off the enemy's attacks, these exotic technologies are unlike anything the Tech-Priests can replicate.
6	**Techno-arcana Part:** These bizarre relics, once empowered, interact with the Machine God's faithful in unusual ways, their spirits responding to certain, holy cant.

Assembling Archeotech Treasures

When you have collected enough archeotech parts, you can assemble them into a powerful item using the Assemble Archeotech Requisition (pg 74). In order to assemble an item you need one power source and one of the following:

- One weapon part.
- One force field part.
- One techno-arcana part.

When assembling an archeotech weapon, that weapon's name is the combination of the power source's name and the weapon part's name. The weapon's profile is a combination of that weapon part's profile and the weapon ability granted by that power source. Archeotech weapons cannot be upgraded by Weapon Enhancements (see the Warhammer 40,000 Core Book).

Example: Joe assembles an archeotech weapon using the acidic conductor power source and electro-fused vambraces weapon part. He creates the following weapon:

WEAPON	RANGE	TYPE	S	AP	D
Acidic conductor electro-fused vambraces	Assault 8	18"	3	-1	1

Abilities: The bearer can only shoot with this weapon once per battle. Each time an attack is made with this weapon, an unmodified wound roll of 6 inflicts D3 mortal wounds on the target in addition to any normal damage.

When assembling an archeotech force field, that force field's name is the combination of the power source's name and the force field part's name. The bearer gains an ability based on the combination of that force field part's ability and the force field ability granted by that power source.

Example: Joe assembles an archeotech force field using the acidic conductor power source and technodermis force field part. He creates the following force field:

Acidic conductor technodermis: Add 1 to the Toughness characteristic of the bearer. The bearer gains the following ability: '**Acid-hardened Flesh (Aura):** While a friendly **<FORGE WORLD> CORE** unit is within 6" of this model, each time a melee attack with an Armour Penetration characteristic of -1 is allocated to a model in that unit, that attack has an Armour Penetration characteristic of 0 instead.'

When assembling an archeotech techno-arcana, that techno-arcana's name is the combination of the power source's name and the techno-arcana part's name. The bearer gains an ability based on the combination of that techno-arcana part's ability and the techno-arcana effect granted by that power source.

Example: Joe assembles an archeotech techno-arcana using the induction node power source and obscuroptikon techno-arcana part. He creates the following techno-arcana:

Obscuroptikon induction node: When the Shroudpsalm Canticle (pg 85) becomes active for your army, you can choose to use this techno-arcana. If you do so, until the end of the battle round, this piece of techno-arcana is active and, until the end of the battle, no other piece of techno-arcana from your army can be used. The bearer gains the following ability: '**Electrified Actuators (Aura):** While a friendly **<FORGE WORLD> CULT MECHANICUS** unit is within 6" of this model, if this techno-arcana is active, each time that unit Advances, do not make an Advance roll. Instead, until the end of the phase, add D3+3" to the Move characteristic of models in that unit.'

When a piece of archeotech is assembled, remove the parts that were used to assemble it from your Order of Battle and select one **ADEPTUS MECHANICUS TECH-PRIEST** unit from your Crusade Force. That unit adds that piece of archeotech to their personal archeotech collection and its Crusade points are increased by 1, make a note on that unit's Crusade Card.

When you are mustering your army, each **ADEPTUS MECHANICUS TECH-PRIEST** unit from your army can be equipped with:

- 1 archeotech force field from their collection.
- 1 archeotech weapon from their collection.
- 1 archeotech techno-arcana from their collection.

POWER SOURCES

1. RESTRAINED VORTEX

Vortex technology uses immense energies to punch a hole through the skein of reality.

WEAPON ABILITY:

After the bearer has shot with this weapon, select one enemy unit that was hit by an attack made with this weapon. Roll one D6 for each other unit within 3" of the target, subtracting 1 if that unit has the **CHARACTER** keyword: on a 3-5, that unit suffers 1 mortal wound; on a 6, that unit suffers D3 mortal wounds.

FORCE FIELD ABILITY

The bearer gains the following ability: '**Vortex Field (Aura):** While a friendly **<FORGE WORLD> CORE** unit is within 6" of this model, each time an enemy unit declares a charge against that unit, if that friendly unit is not within Engagement Range of any enemy units, it can Hold Steady or Set to Defend.'

TECHNO-ARCANA EFFECT:

The bearer gains the following ability: '**Repellent Energies (Aura):** While a friendly **<FORGE WORLD> CULT MECHANICUS** unit is within 6" of this model, if this techno-arcana is active, each time an enemy unit makes a melee attack against that unit, that attack's hit roll cannot be re-rolled and that attack's wound roll cannot be re-rolled.'

2. SPATIAL ALTERNATOR

Based upon grav-field manipulation, this technology condenses or disperses molecular alignment.

WEAPON ABILITY:

Each time a model in an enemy unit (excluding **VEHICLE** units) loses one or more wounds as a result of an attack made with this weapon, roll one D6: on a 4+, until the start of your next Command phase, that unit is condensed. While a unit is condensed, it loses the Objective Secured ability (this ability is described in the Warhammer 40,000 Core Book).

FORCE FIELD ABILITY:

Add 1 to the bearer's Wounds characteristic.

TECHNO-ARCANA EFFECT:

The bearer gains the following ability: '**Spatial Adjustment (Aura):** While a friendly **<FORGE WORLD> CULT MECHANICUS** unit is within 6" of this model, if this techno-arcana is active, each time a ranged attack with an Armour Penetration characteristic of -1 is allocated to a model in that unit while it is receiving the benefits of Light cover from a terrain feature, that attack has an Armour Penetration characteristic of 0 instead.'

3. TELEPORTATION MATRIX

This device enables energy and matter to translocate instantaneously.

WEAPON ABILITY:

Once per battle, after the bearer has shot with this weapon, if it successfully hit an enemy unit when making any of those attacks, it can engage the teleportation grapple. If it does so, remove the bearer from the battlefield, then set the bearer back up on the battlefield anywhere that is within Engagement Range of that enemy unit, and not within Engagement Range of any other enemy units. The bearer counts as having made a charge move this turn.

FORCE FIELD ABILITY:

The bearer is eligible to perform a Heroic Intervention if it is within 6" horizontally and 5" vertically of any enemy unit. Each time the bearer makes a Heroic Intervention move, it can move up to 6" instead of 3". All other rules for Heroic Interventions still apply.

TECHNO-ARCANA EFFECT:

The bearer gains the following ability: '**Aggressive Translocation (Aura):** While a friendly **<FORGE WORLD> CULT MECHANICUS** unit is within 6" of this model, if this techno-arcana is active, you can re-roll charge rolls made for that unit.'

4. ACIDIC CONDUCTOR

Through arcane distillation this technology can eat through metal, dissipate thick smog and even cause genetic scarification.

WEAPON ABILITY:

Each time an attack is made with this weapon, an unmodified wound roll of 6 inflicts D3 mortal wounds on the target in addition to any normal damage.

FORCE FIELD ABILITY:

The bearer gains the following ability: '**Acid-hardened Flesh (Aura):** While a friendly **<FORGE WORLD> CORE** unit is within 6" of this model, each time a melee attack with an Armour Penetration characteristic of -1 is allocated to a model in that unit, that attack has an Armour Penetration characteristic of 0 instead.'

TECHNO-ARCANA EFFECT:

The bearer gains the following ability: '**Haze-devouring Condensate (Aura):** While a friendly **<FORGE WORLD> CULT MECHANICUS** unit is within 6" of this model, if this techno-arcana is active, add 3" to the Range characteristic of ranged weapons models in that unit are equipped with.'

5. ENDOTHERMIC REACTOR

This crystal lattice produces freezing temperatures, its power bleeding the energy and momentum from those it touches.

WEAPON ABILITY:

Each time an attack is made with this weapon, if the attack successfully hits the target, roll one D6, subtracting 1 if the target has the **VEHICLE** keyword: on a 3+, until the start of your next Command phase, the target is frozen. While a unit is frozen, halve the Move characteristic of models in that unit.

FORCE FIELD ABILITY:

Each time the bearer is declared as a target of a charge, subtract 2 from that charge roll.

TECHNO-ARCANA EFFECT:

The bearer gains the following ability: '**Dispersed Cryo-sweep (Aura):** While a friendly **<FORGE WORLD> CULT MECHANICUS** unit is within 6" of this model, at the start of the Fight phase, if this techno-arcana is active and that unit is within Engagement Range of any enemy units, it can fight first that phase.

6. INDUCTION NODE

The electrical purity of the Motive Force fries delicate systems and invigorates the blessed augmentations of the Cult's faithful.

WEAPON ABILITY:

Each time a model in an enemy **VEHICLE** unit loses one or more wounds as a result of an attack made with this weapon, roll one D6: on a 3+, randomly determine one ranged weapon that model is equipped with. Until the start of your next Command phase, each time that model shoots, it makes 1 less attack with that weapon.

FORCE FIELD ABILITY:

The bearer gains the following ability: '**Over-amped Systems (Aura):** While a friendly **<FORGE WORLD> CORE** unit is within 6" of this model, each time that unit shoots or fights, when resolving its attacks you can re-roll one hit roll or one wound roll.'

TECHNO-ARCANA EFFECT:

The bearer gains the following ability: '**Electrified Actuators (Aura):** While a friendly **<FORGE WORLD> CULT MECHANICUS** unit is within 6" of this model, if this techno-arcana is active, each time that unit Advances, do not make an Advance roll. Instead, until the end of the phase, add D3+3" to the Move characteristic of models in that unit.'

WEAPON PARTS

1. ELECTRO-FIRE IMPLANTS

This weapon has the following profile:

WEAPON	RANGE	TYPE	S	AP	D
Electro-fire Implants	12"	Assault D3+3	5	-1	2

Abilities: The bearer can only shoot with this weapon once per battle. Each time an attack is made with this weapon, that attack automatically hits the target.

2. NEURAL JAMMER

This weapon has the following profile:

WEAPON	RANGE	TYPE	S	AP	D
Neural jammer	18"	Pistol 4	4	-2	1

Abilities: The bearer can only shoot with this weapon once per battle. Each time you select a target for this weapon, you can ignore the Look Out, Sir rule. Each time an attack is made with this weapon, an unmodified wound roll of 6 inflicts 1 mortal wound on the target in addition to any normal damage.

3. NANOSHARD PROJECTOR

This weapon has the following profile:

WEAPON	RANGE	TYPE	S	AP	D
Nanoshard projector	12"	Pistol 3	5	-2	2

Abilities: The bearer can only shoot with this weapon once per battle. Each time an attack is made with this weapon, an unmodified hit roll of 6 scores 1 additional hit.

4. ARC ANNULUS

This weapon has the following profile:

WEAPON	RANGE	TYPE	S	AP	D
Arc annulus	18"	Pistol 2	7	-2	2

Abilities: The bearer can only shoot with this weapon once per battle. Each time an attack is made with this weapon against a **Vehicle** unit, that attack has a Damage characteristic of 3 and an unmodified wound roll of 4+ successfully wounds the target.

5. ELECTRO-FUSED VAMBRACES

This weapon has the following profile:

WEAPON	RANGE	TYPE	S	AP	D
Electro-fused vambraces	18"	Assault 8	3	-1	1

Abilities: The bearer can only shoot with this weapon once per battle.

6. DIGITAL CANNON

This weapon has the following profile:

WEAPON	RANGE	TYPE	S	AP	D
Digital cannon	24"	Assault 2	6	-1	3

Abilities: The bearer can only shoot with this weapon once per battle.

FORCE FIELD PARTS

1. VOID SHELL

Each time the bearer would lose a wound, roll one D6: on a 6, that wound is not lost.

2. ARC IMPLANTS

At the start of the Fight phase, select one enemy unit within Engagement Range of the bearer and roll one D6: on a 2-5, that enemy unit suffers 1 mortal wound; on a 6, it suffers D3 mortal wounds.

3. TIME SINK

At the start of the Fight phase, select one enemy model within Engagement Range of the bearer. Roll one D6 and add the bearer's Leadership characteristic to the result. Your opponent rolls one D6 and adds that enemy model's Leadership characteristic to their result. If your total is greater than your opponent's, until the end of the phase, that enemy model's unit is not eligible to fight until after all eligible units from your army have done so.

4. CONVERSION ERADICATOR

When the bearer is destroyed, roll one D6: on a 2-5, the nearest enemy unit within 6" suffers D3 mortal wounds; on a 6, the nearest enemy unit within 6" suffers 2D3 mortal wounds.

5. INVERSE POWER FEEDS

Each time the bearer makes a melee attack, an unmodified wound roll of 6 inflicts 1 mortal wound on the target in addition to any normal damage.

6. TECHNODERMIS

Add 1 to the Toughness characteristic of the bearer.

TECHNO-ARCANA PARTS

1. OBSCUROPTIKON

When the Shroudpsalm Canticle (pg 85) becomes active for your army, you can choose to use this techno-arcana. If you do so, until the end of the battle round, this piece of techno-arcana is active and, until the end of the battle, no other piece of techno-arcana from your army can be used.

2. EXO-GAUNTLET

When the Chant of the Remorseless Fist Canticle (pg 85) becomes active for your army, you can choose to use this techno-arcana. If you do so, until the end of the battle round, this piece of techno-arcana is active and, until the end of the battle, no other piece of techno-arcana from your army can be used.

3. FERROSANCTIC ORRERY

When the Incantation of the Iron Soul Canticle becomes active for your army, you can choose to use this techno-arcana. If you do so, until the end of the battle round, this piece of techno-arcana is active and, until the end of the battle, no other piece of techno-arcana from your army can be used.

4. HAGIOSCOPE

When the Benediction of the Omnissiah Canticle (pg 85) becomes active for your army, you can choose to use this techno-arcana. If you do so, until the end of the battle round, this piece of techno-arcana is active and, until the end of the battle, no other piece of techno-arcana from your army can be used.

5. TRI-DIMENSIONAL COVENANT

When the Invocation of Machine Vengeance Canticle (pg 85) becomes active for your army, you can choose to use this techno-arcana. If you do so, until the end of the battle round, this piece of techno-arcana is active and, until the end of the battle, no other piece of techno-arcana from your army can be used.

6. HYPERCIRCUIT

When the Litany of the Electromancer Canticle (pg 85) becomes active for your army, you can choose to use this techno-arcana. If you do so, until the end of the battle round, this piece of techno-arcana is active and, until the end of the battle, no other piece of techno-arcana from your army can be used.

Dawn breaks through pestilential mists on a world designated K82401-b by a crusading Explorator fleet. Among the ruins of Human habitation, the fleet's vanguard repels daemonic harbingers that stalk from strange growths coating the ruins.

CRUSADE ARMY

Sometimes, the initial theme for a Crusade Force can provide ideas for selecting the first wave of troops, with the force's unfolding story providing more depth as its campaign progresses. This was certainly the case with senior graphic designer Joel Martin's collection.

Joel's Crusade Force represents a portion of an Explorator fleet dispatched from Mars by Belisarius Cawl. Under the leadership of his Tech-Priest Manipulus, Xixos-117, he sees them as undertaking the Quest for Knowledge, seeking out lost archeotech and retrieving stolen relics from the clutches of heretic cultists and vile xenos. The selection of units to form his starting force was intended to reflect the fleet's 'forward' elements; those that scout ahead, searching for rumours of ancient technology and probing the enemy's forces for weaknesses.

Joel's initial forces are the ones to make the first strikes and, if need be, call in the more elite, specialised and armoured elements of the fleet, such as Pteraxii or Kastelan Robots. These powerful units are at the top of his list to add to his growing force once Requisition Points start building up and his tally of battles begins to forge a unique narrative. For now, Joel wanted to include a mix of units with different capabilities that would both suit his play style and be really fun to use on the tabletop. He has a core of Skitarii Vanguard and Rangers, whose inclusion is based not only on their in-game abilities, but also because he loves their sculpts.

The Adeptus Mechanicus has access to a host of destructive ranged weaponry, but Joel was keen to not leave his force as a static gunline army – after all, they are meant to push forward the boundaries of Mars' influence. To this end, he has added units of zealous Fulgurite Electro-Priests and blade-wielding Sicarian Ruststalkers, which he uses both to project the Machine God's power further onto the battlefield and to defend his core infantry and war engine from any enemies that attempt to get too close.

Joel has always enjoyed painting vehicles to add to his armies. The large surfaces of an Onager Dunecrawler and Skorpius Dunerider gave him the opportunity to add weathering details and battle damage. He used a sponge to achieve some of these effects and painted on small chips in silver to show the metal beneath the Martian livery. To create rust effects, Joel's tip is to create a mix of Mournfang Brown and Lahmian Medium to serve as a wash. He applied this around rivets and armour joints, and found it's a great way to add further depth to purely metallic areas. He decided to keep to a bold colour scheme and a limited palette, using a bright blue for power coils and lights to stand out as an accent colour against the oily metalics and deep, Martian red.

DATASHEETS

This section contains the datasheets that you will need to fight battles with your Adeptus Mechanicus miniatures, as well as details of army-specific abilities. You can find out how to use datasheets in the Warhammer 40,000 Core Book.

THE <FORGE WORLD> KEYWORD

Many datasheets in this section have the <FORGE WORLD> keyword. This is a keyword that you can select for yourself, as described in the Warhammer 40,000 Core Book, with the guidance detailed below.

Adeptus Mechanicus units are drawn from a Forge World. When you include such a unit in your army, you must nominate which Forge World it is from and then replace the <FORGE WORLD> keyword in every instance on its datasheet with the name of your chosen Forge World. This could be one of the Forge Worlds detailed in a Warhammer 40,000 publication, or one of your own design.

> **Example:** *If you include a Tech-Priest Dominus in your army, and you decide he is from the Ryza Forge World, his* <FORGE WORLD> *keyword becomes* RYZA *and his Lord of the Machine Cult ability reads, 'While a friendly* RYZA CORE *unit is within 6" of this model, each time a model in that unit makes an attack, re-roll a hit roll of 1.'*

If your army is Battle-forged, you cannot include units from two different Forge Worlds in the same Detachment. You can find out more about Battle-forged armies in the Warhammer 40,000 Core Book.

WEAPON PROFILES

The weapon profiles found on a unit's datasheet describe the primary weapons that models in that unit can be equipped with. Some weapons are only referenced on a datasheet; profiles for these, and all other weapons, can be found on pages 112-115.

ABILITIES

A unit's datasheet will list all the abilities it has. Certain abilities that are common to many units are only referenced on the datasheets rather than described in full. These abilities are described below.

Doctrina Imperatives

If every unit from your army has the ADEPTUS MECHANICUS keyword (excluding AGENT OF THE IMPERIUM, UNALIGNED and KNIGHT OF THE COG units), this unit's characteristics are modified depending on which Doctrina Imperative is active for your army. Each Doctrina Imperative has two effects, an Optimisation effect that improves one of this unit's characteristics, and a Deprecation effect that reduces one of this unit's characteristics. When a Doctrina Imperative is active, both of these effects will apply to this unit.

At the start of the battle round, if there is a DOCTRINA ASSEMBLER model from your army on the battlefield, you can select one Doctrina Imperative that has not yet been active for your army. If you do so, until the end of the battle round, that Doctrina Imperative is active for your army.

Canticles of the Omnissiah

If every unit from your army has the ADEPTUS MECHANICUS keyword (excluding AGENT OF THE IMPERIUM, UNALIGNED and KNIGHT OF THE COG units), this unit gains a bonus depending on which Canticle of the Omnissiah is active for your army.

At the start of the battle round, you can select one Canticle that has not yet been active for your army. If you do so, until the end of the battle round, that Canticle is active for your army.

DOCTRINA IMPERATIVES

PROTECTOR IMPERATIVE

The Protector imperative is codified to yield the maximum spectra of hard data. Extra power is fed into narrow-band optics and rangefinders connected directly to the Skitarii's priority programming as the holy warriors' guns become an extension of themselves.

OPTIMISATION

Improve the Ballistic Skill characteristic of models in this unit by 1.

DEPRECATION

Reduce the Weapon Skill characteristic of models in this unit by 1.

CONQUEROR IMPERATIVE

When the enemy close in, the Tech-Priests controlling each maniple inload Conqueror imperatives that boost the martial subroutines of their Skitarii minions and galvanise them into physical action at the expense of their more elaborate targeting programmes.

OPTIMISATION

Improve the Weapon Skill characteristic of models in this unit by 1.

DEPRECATION

Reduce the Ballistic Skill characteristic of models in this unit by 1.

BULWARK IMPERATIVE

The warrior wisdom of ancient and experienced Reductors is force-loaded into the Skitarii's minds. Each thrilling pulse of data locks microactuators into bracing positions, brings reserve power cells online and bestows a sensation of sacred invulnerability upon the Tech-Priests' soldiers.

OPTIMISATION

Improve the Save characteristic of models in this unit by 1 (models in this unit cannot have a Save characteristic better than 2+).

DEPRECATION

Reduce the Move characteristic of models in this unit by 3".

AGGRESSOR IMPERATIVE

The Skitarii feel the press of an invisible hand upon their minds as the Machine God drives them forward. Servos are pushed to their structural limits as fibre bundles fill with the boundless energy of the Motive Force and propel the faithful on an unstoppable crusade.

OPTIMISATION

Improve the Move characteristic of models in this unit by 3".

DEPRECATION

Reduce the Save characteristic of models in this unit by 1.

CANTICLES OF THE OMNISSIAH

SHROUDPSALM

Robot, servitor and priest shift their binharic emissions into visible spectra, the static pouring from their vox-grilles manifesting as an electromagnetic storm that hides them from the foe.

While this Canticle is active, this unit counts as receiving the benefits of Light Cover.

CHANT OF THE REMORSELESS FIST

In spitting out a staccato chant to the Motive Force, the faithful warriors of the Cult Mechanicus are filled with merciless surety as well as intent.

While this Canticle is active, each time a model in this unit make a melee attack, add 1 to the Strength characteristic of that attack.

INCANTATION OF THE IRON SOUL

Raising their voices in binharic praise, the Disciples of the Machine God bolster their spirits with the surety of iron.

While this Canticle is active:

- Each time a Combat Attrition test is taken for this unit, ignore any or all modifiers.
- Each time a model in this unit would lose a wound as a result of a mortal wound, roll one D6: on a 5+, that wound is not lost. If this unit has the Refusal to Yield dogma, that wound is not lost on a 4+ instead.

BENEDICTION OF THE OMNISSIAH

Those blessed enough to comprehend this blaring vox-prayer find their targeting reticules guided by the Omnissiah's own vigilance.

While this Canticle is active, each time this unit is selected to shoot, when resolving its attacks you can:

- Re-roll one hit roll.
- Re-roll one wound roll.
- Re-roll one damage roll.

INVOCATION OF MACHINE VENGEANCE

The Tech-Priests lead adherents of the Machine Cult in a binharic prayer of hatred against the unenlightened. A manifestation of power surges through tendons, wires and pistons as the righteous eagerly close on the blasphemers.

While this Canticle is active, each time an Advance roll or a charge roll is made for this unit, roll one additional D6 and discard the lowest result.

LITANY OF THE ELECTROMANCER

Summoning the spark of the Machine God's divinity that burns within them, the Omnissiah's faithful manifest auras of energy that disrupt the unbeliever's neuro-cortices and cause the foe to spasm.

While this Canticle is active, each time a melee attack is made against this unit, subtract 1 from that attack's hit roll.

Belisarius Cawl's war form is a multi-limbed, bio-mechanical hybrid. Advanced bionics grant him immense strength and resilience, while snaking tendrils rapidly repair his cybernetic body. For 10,000 years, Cawl has eradicated the Imperium's enemies, and he leads the Machine God's devotees in holy acquisition still.

BELISARIUS CAWL

9 POWER

No.	Name	M	WS	BS	S	T	W	A	Ld	Sv
1	Belisarius Cawl	6"	2+	2+	5	6	8	4	9	2+

Belisarius Cawl is equipped with: solar atomiser; arc scourge; mechadendrite hive; Omnissian axe. Your army can only include one **BELISARIUS CAWL** model.

WEAPON	RANGE	TYPE	S	AP	D	ABILITIES
Solar atomiser	12"	Assault D3	10	-4	3	Blast. Each time an attack made with this weapon targets a unit within half range, that attack has a Damage characteristic of D3+3.
Arc scourge	Melee	Melee	x2	-2	1	Each time an attack is made with this weapon against a **VEHICLE** unit, that attack has a Damage characteristic of 2 and an unmodified wound roll of 2+ successfully wounds the target.
Mechadendrite hive	Melee	Melee	User	0	1	Each time the bearer fights, it makes 2D6 additional attacks with this weapon.
Omnissian axe	Melee	Melee	+2	-2	2	-

ABILITIES

Canticles of the Omnissiah (pg 84-85)

Refractor Field: This model has a 5+ invulnerable save.

Lord of the Machine Cult (Aura): While a friendly **ADEPTUS MECHANICUS CORE** unit is within 6" of this model, each time a model in that unit makes an attack, re-roll a hit roll of 1.

Lord of Mars: In your Command phase, select one friendly **MARS CORE** unit within 6" of this model. Until the start of your next Command phase, each time a model in that unit makes an attack, you can re-roll the hit roll.

Lead in Prayer: In your Command phase, you can select one friendly **CULT MECHANICUS CORE** unit within 6" of this model. If you do so, then select one Canticle (pg 85) – this can be one that has already been active for your army. Until the start of your next Command phase, both this model and that unit benefit from the selected Canticle instead of the one that is active for your army.

Master of Machines: At the end of your Movement phase, this model can repair one other friendly **ADEPTUS MECHANICUS** or **IMPERIUM VEHICLE** model within 3" of it. That model regains up to D3 lost wounds. Each model can only be repaired once per turn.

Self-repair Mechanisms: In your Command phase, this model can repair itself. If it does so, it regains up to D3 lost wounds. Each model can only be repaired once per turn.

FACTION KEYWORDS: **IMPERIUM, ADEPTUS MECHANICUS, CULT MECHANICUS, MARS**
KEYWORDS: **MONSTER, CHARACTER, SUPREME COMMANDER, DOCTRINA ASSEMBLER, TECH-PRIEST, BELISARIUS CAWL**

TECH-PRIEST MANIPULUS

4 POWER

No.	Name	M	WS	BS	S	T	W	A	Ld	Sv
1	Tech-Priest Manipulus	6"	3+	2+	4	4	5	3	8	2+

A Tech-Priest Manipulus is equipped with: magnarail lance; Manipulus mechadendrites; Omnissian staff.

WEAPON	RANGE	TYPE	S	AP	D	ABILITIES
Magnarail lance	36"	Heavy 1	7	-3	3	-
Transonic cannon	12"	Assault D6	4	-1	2	Each time an attack is made with this weapon, that attack automatically hits the target. Each time an attack is made with this weapon, an unmodified wound roll of 6 inflicts 1 mortal wound on the target in addition to any normal damage.
Manipulus mechadendrites	Melee	Melee	User	0	1	Each time the bearer fights, it makes 3 additional attacks with this weapon.
Omnissian staff	Melee	Melee	+3	-1	2	-

WARGEAR OPTIONS

- This model's magnarail lance can be replaced with 1 transonic cannon.

ABILITIES

Canticles of the Omnissiah (pg 84-85)

Master of Machines: At the end of your Movement phase, this model can repair one friendly <Forge World> model within 3" of it. That model regains up to D3 lost wounds. Each model can only be repaired once per turn.

Refractor Field: This model has a 5+ invulnerable save.

Galvanic Field: In your Command phase, select one friendly <Forge World> Core unit within 9" of this model. Until the start of your next Command phase, add 6" to the range of Galvanic, Arc and Radium weapons (pg 112) models in that unit are equipped with (excluding Grenade weapons) and each time an attack is made with one of those weapons, the Armour Penetration characteristic of that attack is improved by 1.

Among the augmentations of a Tech-Priest Manipulus is a galvanic cell from which they channel powerful charges of the Motive Force. They drain power sources dry and use the energy to overcharge the cells of their warriors' armaments, all while defending their divine work with blasts from their own arcane weapons.

FACTION KEYWORDS: Imperium, Adeptus Mechanicus, Cult Mechanicus, <Forge World>
KEYWORDS: Infantry, Character, Doctrina Assembler, Tech-Priest, Tech-Priest Manipulus

TECH-PRIEST DOMINUS

4 POWER

No.	Name	M	WS	BS	S	T	W	A	Ld	Sv
1	Tech-Priest Dominus	6"	3+	2+	4	4	5	3	8	2+

A Tech-Priest Dominus is equipped with: macrostubber; volkite blaster; Omnissian axe.

WEAPON	RANGE	TYPE	S	AP	D	ABILITIES
Eradication ray	Before selecting targets, select one of the profiles below to make attacks with.					
- Focused	12"	Heavy D3	6	-3	2	Blast
- Dissipated	24"	Heavy D3	6	-2	1	Blast
Macrostubber	12"	Pistol 5	4	0	1	-
Phosphor serpenta	18"	Assault 1	5	-1	1	Each time an attack is made with this weapon, the target does not receive the benefits of Dense Cover against that attack.
Volkite blaster	24"	Heavy 3	6	0	2	Each time an attack is made with this weapon, an unmodified wound roll of 6 inflicts 2 mortal wounds on the target in addition to any normal damage.
Omnissian axe	Melee	Melee	+2	-2	2	-

WARGEAR OPTIONS

- This model's macrostubber can be replaced with 1 phosphor serpenta.
- This model's volkite blaster can be replaced with 1 eradication ray.

ABILITIES

Canticles of the Omnissiah (pg 84-85)

Master of Machines: At the end of your Movement phase, this model can repair one friendly <Forge World> model within 3" of it. That model regains up to D3 lost wounds. Each model can only be repaired once per turn.

Refractor Field: This model has a 5+ invulnerable save.

Lord of the Machine Cult (Aura): While a friendly <Forge World> Core unit is within 6" of this model, each time a model in that unit makes an attack, re-roll a hit roll of 1.

FACTION KEYWORDS: **Imperium, Adeptus Mechanicus, Cult Mechanicus, <Forge World>**
KEYWORDS: **Infantry, Character, Doctrina Assembler, Tech-Priest, Tech-Priest Dominus**

Tech-Priests Dominus are the theocratic generals of a forge world's armies. They lead congregation of warriors in binharic prayer and direct those beneath them with precision strategies. They are masters of machines, as capable of healing damage to their creations as they are at destroying the enemy's corrupted engines.

TECHNOARCHEOLOGIST

3 POWER

No.	Name	M	WS	BS	S	T	W	A	Ld	Sv
1	Technoarcheologist	6"	4+	3+	4	4	4	2	8	3+

A Technoarcheologist is equipped with: eradication pistol; servo-arc claw.

WEAPON	RANGE	TYPE	S	AP	D	ABILITIES
Eradication pistol	Before selecting targets, select one of the profiles below to make attacks with.					
- Focused	6"	Pistol D3	6	-3	2	Blast
- Dissipated	12"	Pistol D3	6	-2	1	Blast
Servo-arc claw	Melee	Melee	+3	-2	3	Each time the bearer fights, no more than one attack can be made with each servo-arc claw. Each time an attack is made with this weapon against a **VEHICLE** unit, that attack has a Damage characteristic of 4 and an unmodified wound roll of 4+ successfully wounds the target.

ABILITIES

Canticles of the Omnissiah (pg 84-85)

Enhanced Bionics: This model has a 5+ invulnerable save.

Omni-scrambler: Enemy units that are set up on the battlefield as Reinforcements cannot be set up within 12" of this unit.

Brotherhood of the Cog: If your army is Battle-forged, then for each **TECH-PRIEST DOMINUS** or **TECH-PRIEST MANIPULUS** unit included in a Detachment, one **TECH-PRIEST ENGINSEER** or **TECHNOARCHEOLOGIST** unit can be included in that Detachment without taking up an additional Battlefield Role slot.

Machine Focus: In your Command phase, select one friendly **<FORGE WORLD> CORE**, **<FORGE WORLD> KATAPHRON SERVITORS** or **<FORGE WORLD> SERVITORS** unit within 6" of this model. Until the start of your next Command phase:

- If that unit has the **KATAPHRON SERVITORS** keyword, it can perform actions as if it had the **INFANTRY** keyword.

- While that unit is performing an action, it can make ranged attacks without that action failing.

Master of Machines: At the end of your Movement phase, this model can repair one friendly **<FORGE WORLD>** model within 3" of it. That model regains up to D3 lost wounds. Each model can only be repaired once per turn.

FACTION KEYWORDS: **IMPERIUM, ADEPTUS MECHANICUS, CULT MECHANICUS, <FORGE WORLD>**

KEYWORDS: **INFANTRY, CHARACTER, DOCTRINA ASSEMBLER, TECH-PRIEST, TECHNOARCHEOLOGIST**

Technoarcheologists are seekers of divine arcana, driven to uncover that which is hidden and to analyse its capabilities. Hardened to life on the Imperium's dangerous frontiers, these priests employ cogitative instincts to detect approaching foes and awaken their servitor guardians to effective modes of attack.

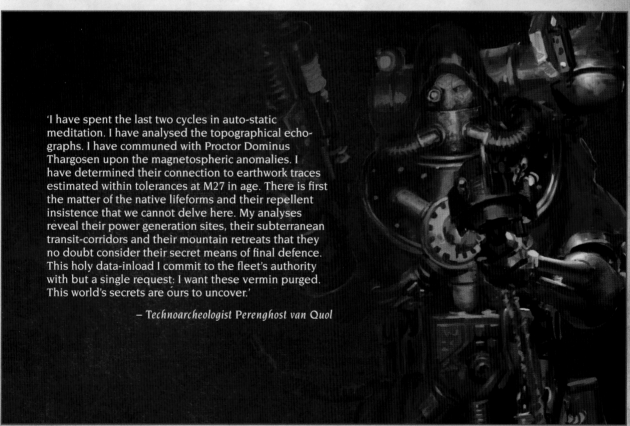

'I have spent the last two cycles in auto-static meditation. I have analysed the topographical echo-graphs. I have communed with Proctor Dominus Thargosen upon the magnetospheric anomalies. I have determined their connection to earthwork traces estimated within tolerances at M27 in age. There is first the matter of the native lifeforms and their repellent insistence that we cannot delve here. My analyses reveal their power generation sites, their subterranean transit-corridors and their mountain retreats that they no doubt consider their secret means of final defence. This holy data-inload I commit to the fleet's authority with but a single request: I want these vermin purged. This world's secrets are ours to uncover.'

– *Technoarcheologist Perenghost van Quol*

SKITARII MARSHAL

3 POWER

No.	Name	M	WS	BS	S	T	W	A	Ld	Sv
1	Skitarii Marshal	6"	3+	2+	3	3	4	3	8	4+

A Skitarii Marshal is equipped with: radium serpenta; control stave.

WEAPON	RANGE	TYPE	S	AP	D	ABILITIES
Radium serpenta	18"	Assault 1	3	0	1	Each time an attack is made with this weapon against an enemy unit (excluding **Vehicle** units), an unmodified hit roll of 6 automatically wounds the target.
Control stave	Melee	Melee	+3	-2	1	-

ABILITIES

Doctrina Imperatives (see pg 85)

Control Edict: In your Command phase, you can select one friendly <**Forge World**> **Skitarii** unit within 9" of this model or you can select one friendly <**Forge World**> **Skitarii Data-tether** unit anywhere on the battlefield. Until the start of your next Command phase, that unit ignores the Deprecation effect of the currently active Doctrina Imperative.

Servo-skull Uplink (Aura): While a friendly <**Forge World**> **Skitarii Core** unit is within 6" of this model, each time a model in that unit makes an attack, re-roll a wound roll of 1.

Enhanced Bionics: This model has a 5+ invulnerable save.

FACTION KEYWORDS: **Imperium, Adeptus Mechanicus, Skitarii, <Forge World>**
KEYWORDS: **Infantry, Character, Doctrina Assembler, Skitarii Marshal**

Marshals lead the maniples and cohorts of Skitarii soldiery. They are veteran warriors of countless crusades, privileged to bear enhanced augmentations. Marshals stand as intermediaries between Skitarii formations and their priestly masters, employing sacred uplinks to refine their warriors' doctrines closer to holy perfection.

TECH-PRIEST ENGINSEER

3 POWER

No.	Name	M	WS	BS	S	T	W	A	Ld	Sv
1	Tech-Priest Enginseer	6"	4+	3+	4	4	4	2	8	3+

A Tech-Priest Enginseer is equipped with: Mechanicus pistol; Omnissian axe; servo-arm.

WEAPON	RANGE	TYPE	S	AP	D	ABILITIES
Mechanicus pistol	12"	Pistol 2	4	-2	1	-
Omnissian axe	Melee	Melee	+2	-2	2	-
Servo-arm	Melee	Melee	x2	-2	3	Each time the bearer fights, no more than one attack can be made with each servo-arm.

ABILITIES

Canticles of the Omnissiah (pg 84-85)

Enhanced Bionics: This model has a 5+ invulnerable save.

Master of Machines: At the end of your Movement phase, this model can repair one friendly <FORGE WORLD> model within 3" of it. That model regains up to D3 lost wounds. Each model can only be repaired once per turn.

Awaken the Machine: In your Command phase, this model can awaken one friendly <FORGE WORLD> VEHICLE model (excluding KASTELAN ROBOT models) within 3"of it. Until the start of your next Command phase, each time that model makes an attack, add 1 to that attack's hit roll. Each model can only be awakened once per turn.

Brotherhood of the Cog: If your army is Battle-forged, then for each TECH-PRIEST DOMINUS or TECH-PRIEST MANIPULUS unit included in a Detachment, one TECH-PRIEST ENGINSEER or TECHNO ARCAEOLOGIST unit can be included in that Detachment without taking up an additional Battlefield Role slot.

FACTION KEYWORDS: IMPERIUM, ADEPTUS MECHANICUS, CULT MECHANICUS, <FORGE WORLD>

KEYWORDS: INFANTRY, CHARACTER, DOCTRINA ASSEMBLER, TECH-PRIEST, TECH-PRIEST ENGINSEER

The most widespread of a forge world's priesthood, Enginseers maintain many of the Imperium's mechanisms, such as reactors, battle tanks and even starships. They have an intuitive connection with holy apparatuses, and can awaken the most recalcitrant of engine spirits with whispered machine cant.

SKITARII RANGERS

No.	Name	M	WS	BS	S	T	W	A	Ld	Sv
4-19	Skitarii Ranger	6"	4+	3+	3	3	1	1	6	4+
1	Skitarii Ranger Alpha	6"	4+	3+	3	3	1	2	7	4+

If this unit contains between 6 and 10 models, it has **Power Rating 4**. If this unit contains between 11 and 15 models, it has **Power Rating 6**. If this unit contains 16 or more models, it has **Power Rating 8**. Every model is equipped with: galvanic rifle.

WEAPON	RANGE	TYPE	S	AP	D	ABILITIES
Arc rifle	30"	Rapid Fire 1	6	-2	D3	Each time an attack is made with this weapon against a **Vehicle** unit, that attack has a Damage characteristic of 3 and an unmodified wound roll of 4+ successfully wounds the target.
Galvanic rifle	30"	Heavy 2	4	-1	1	-
Plasma caliver	Before selecting targets, select one of the profiles below to make attacks with.					
- Standard	30"	Assault 2	7	-3	1	-
- Supercharge	30"	Assault 2	8	-3	2	If any unmodified hit rolls of 1 are made for attacks with this weapon profile, the bearer is destroyed after shooting with this weapon.
Transuranic arquebus	60"	Heavy 1	7	-2	D3	Each time you select a target for this weapon, you can ignore the Look Out, Sir rule. Each time an attack is made with this weapon, an unmodified wound roll of 6 inflicts 1 mortal wound on the target in addition to any normal damage.

OTHER WARGEAR	ABILITIES
Enhanced data-tether	While the bearer is on the battlefield: • The bearer's unit gains the **Data-tether** keyword. • Add 1 to the Leadership characteristic of models in the bearer's unit.
Omnispex	Each time a model in the bearer's unit makes a ranged attack, the target does not receive the benefits of Light Cover against that attack.

WARGEAR OPTIONS

- If this unit contains 9 or fewer models, 1 Skitarii Ranger's galvanic rifle can be replaced with one of the following: 1 arc rifle; 1 plasma caliver; 1 transuranic arquebus.
- For every 10 models in this unit, 1 Skitarii Ranger's galvanic rifle can be replaced with 1 arc rifle.
- For every 10 models in this unit, 1 Skitarii Ranger's galvanic rifle can be replaced with 1 plasma caliver.
- For every 10 models in this unit, 1 Skitarii Ranger's galvanic rifle can be replaced with 1 transuranic arquebus.
- If this unit contains 9 or fewer models, 1 Skitarii Ranger equipped with a galvanic rifle can be equipped with one of the following: 1 enhanced data-tether; 1 omnispex. That model's galvanic rifle cannot be replaced.
- For every 10 models in this unit, 1 Skitarii Ranger equipped with a galvanic rifle can be equipped with one of the following: 1 enhanced data-tether; 1 omnispex. That model's galvanic rifle cannot be replaced.
- The Skitarii Ranger Alpha can be equipped with one of the following: 1 arc maul; 1 power sword; 1 taser goad.
- The Skitarii Ranger Alpha's galvanic rifle can be replaced with one of the following: 1 arc pistol; 1 phosphor blast pistol; 1 radium pistol.

ABILITIES

Doctrina Imperatives (see pg 85)

Bionics: Models in this unit have a 6+ invulnerable save.

Rangers: At the start of the first battle round, models in this unit can make a Normal Move of up to 3". They cannot end this move within 9" of any enemy models.

FACTION KEYWORDS: Imperium, Adeptus Mechanicus, Skitarii, <Forge World>
KEYWORDS: Infantry, Core, Skitarii Rangers

Rangers relentlessly pursue their quarry over months or even years, tracking their prey unto death. They bear antique, long-barrelled galvanic rifles, whose energised ammunition transfers a coruscating charge when it hits, leaving the prey a smoking husk while the Rangers are already lining up their next target.

SKITARII VANGUARD

2 POWER

No.	Name	M	WS	BS	S	T	W	A	Ld	Sv
4-19	Skitarii Vanguard	6"	4+	3+	3	3	1	1	6	4+
1	Skitarii Vanguard Alpha	6"	4+	3+	3	3	1	2	7	4+

If this unit contains between 6 and 10 models, it has **Power Rating 4**. If this unit contains between 11 and 15 models, it has **Power Rating 6**. If this unit contains 16 or more models, it has **Power Rating 8**. Every model is equipped with: radium carbine.

WEAPON	RANGE	TYPE	S	AP	D	ABILITIES
Arc rifle	30"	Rapid Fire 1	6	-2	D3	Each time an attack is made with this weapon against a **VEHICLE** unit, that attack has a Damage characteristic of 3 and an unmodified wound roll of 4+ successfully wounds the target.
Radium carbine	18"	Assault 3	3	0	1	Each time an attack is made with this weapon against an enemy unit (excluding **VEHICLE** units), an unmodified hit roll of 6 automatically wounds the target.
Plasma caliver	Before selecting targets, select one of the profiles below to make attacks with.					
- Standard	30"	Assault 2	7	-3	1	-
- Supercharge	30"	Assault 2	8	-3	2	If any unmodified hit rolls of 1 are made for attacks with this weapon profile, the bearer is destroyed after shooting with this weapon.
Transuranic arquebus	60"	Heavy 1	7	-2	D3	Each time you select a target for this weapon, you can ignore the Look Out, Sir rule. Each time an attack is made with this weapon, an unmodified wound roll of 6 inflicts 1 mortal wound on the target in addition to any normal damage.

OTHER WARGEAR	ABILITIES
Enhanced data-tether	While the bearer is on the battlefield: • The bearer's unit gains the **DATA-TETHER** keyword. • Add 1 to the Leadership characteristic of models in the bearer's unit.
Omnispex	Each time a model in the bearer's unit makes a ranged attack, the target does not receive the benefits of Light Cover against that attack.

WARGEAR OPTIONS

- If this unit contains 9 or fewer models, 1 Skitarii Vanguard's radium carbine can be replaced with one of the following: 1 arc rifle; 1 plasma caliver; 1 transuranic arquebus.
- For every 10 models in this unit, 1 Skitarii Vanguard's radium carbine can be replaced with 1 arc rifle.
- For every 10 models in this unit, 1 Skitarii Vanguard's radium carbine can be replaced with 1 plasma caliver.
- For every 10 models in this unit, 1 Skitarii Vanguard's radium carbine can be replaced with 1 transuranic arquebus.
- If this unit contains 9 or fewer models, 1 Skitarii Vanguard equipped with a radium carbine can be equipped with one of the following: 1 enhanced data-tether; 1 omnispex. That model's radium carbine cannot be replaced.
- For every 10 models in this unit, 1 Skitarii Vanguard equipped with a radium carbine can be equipped with one of the following: 1 enhanced data-tether; 1 omnispex. That model's radium carbine cannot be replaced.
- The Skitarii Vanguard Alpha can be equipped with one of the following: 1 arc maul; 1 power sword; 1 taser goad.
- The Skitarii Vanguard Alpha's radium carbine can be replaced with one of the following: 1 arc pistol; 1 phosphor blast pistol; 1 radium pistol.

ABILITIES

Doctrina Imperatives (see pg 85)

Bionics: Models in this unit have a 6+ invulnerable save.

Rad-saturation (Aura): While an enemy unit (excluding **VEHICLE** units) is within Engagement Range of this unit, subtract 1 from the Strength and Toughness characteristics of models in that enemy unit.

FACTION KEYWORDS: IMPERIUM, ADEPTUS MECHANICUS, SKITARII, <FORGE WORLD>
KEYWORDS: INFANTRY, CORE, SKITARII VANGUARD

The hyper-irradiated shot unleashed by the Skitarii Vanguard's carbines ensure those that would otherwise survive the injury still sicken and die. Vanguard are infused with this radiation, emitting a debilitating aura they themselves are inured to. This hardens them to fight in the most toxic of war zones to defend the Tech-Priests' interests.

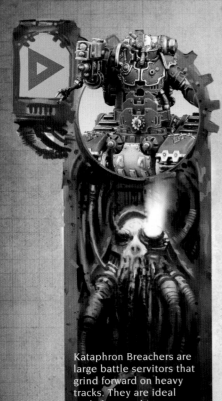

KATAPHRON BREACHERS

6 POWER

No.	Name	M	WS	BS	S	T	W	A	Ld	Sv
3-6	Kataphron Breacher	6"	4+	4+	5	5	3	3	7	2+

If this unit contains 4 or more models, it has **Power Rating 12**. Every model is equipped with: heavy arc rifle; arc claw.

WEAPON	RANGE	TYPE	S	AP	D	ABILITIES
Heavy arc rifle	36"	Heavy 2	6	-2	2	Each time an attack is made with this weapon against a **Vehicle** unit, that attack has a Damage characteristic of 3 and an unmodified wound roll of 4+ successfully wounds the target.
Torsion cannon	48"	Heavy 1	8	-4	D3+3	-
Arc claw	Melee	Melee	+1	-3	1	Each time the bearer fights, it makes 1 additional attack with this weapon. Each time an attack is made with this weapon against a **Vehicle** unit, that attack has a Damage characteristic of 2 and an unmodified wound roll of 4+ successfully wounds the target.
Hydraulic claw	Melee	Melee	x2	-2	3	-

WARGEAR OPTIONS

- Any number of models can each have their heavy arc rifle replaced with 1 torsion cannon.
- Any number of models can each have their arc claw replaced with 1 hydraulic claw.

ABILITIES

Canticles of the Omnissiah (pg 84-85)

Bionics: Models in this unit have a 6+ invulnerable save.

Heavy Battle Servitor: Models in this unit do not suffer the penalty to hit rolls incurred for firing Heavy weapons in the same turn that their unit has moved.

Tracked Mobility: Models in this unit can move through the walls, girders, chains and foliage of terrain features with the Breachable terrain trait (see the Warhammer 40,000 Core Book) without impediment.

FACTION KEYWORDS: Imperium, Adeptus Mechanicus, Cult Mechanicus, <Forge World>
KEYWORDS: Biker, Kataphron Servitors, Kataphron Breachers

Kataphron Breachers are large battle servitors that grind forward on heavy tracks. They are ideal tools for smashing open enemy battle lines and bastions with blasts from heavy weapons and blows from combat attachments, while any enemy firepower is deflected by thick armour and absorbed by layered bionics.

Kataphron Breacher with heavy arc rifle and arc claw

Kataphron Breacher with torsion cannon and hydraulic claw

KATAPHRON DESTROYERS

7 POWER

No.	Name	M	WS	BS	S	T	W	A	Ld	Sv
3-6	Kataphron Destroyer	6"	4+	4+	5	5	3	3	7	3+

If this unit contains 4 or more models, it has **Power Rating 14**. Every model is equipped with: heavy grav-cannon; phosphor blaster.

WEAPON	RANGE	TYPE	S	AP	D	ABILITIES
Cognis flamer	12"	Assault D6+2	4	0	1	Each time an attack is made with this weapon, that attack automatically hits the target.
Heavy grav-cannon	30"	Heavy 5	5	-3	1	Each time an attack made with this weapon is allocated to a model with a Save characteristic of 3+ or better, that attack has a Damage characteristic of 2.
Kataphron plasma culverin	Before selecting targets, select one of the profiles below to make attacks with.					
- Standard	36"	Heavy D6	7	-3	1	Blast
- Supercharge	36"	Heavy D6	8	-3	2	Blast. Each time an unmodified hit roll of 1 is made for an attack with this weapon profile, the bearer's unit suffers 1 mortal wound after shooting with this weapon.
Phosphor blaster	24"	Rapid Fire 1	5	-1	1	Each time an attack is made with this weapon, the target does not receive the benefits of Dense Cover against that attack.

WARGEAR OPTIONS

- Any number of models can each have their heavy grav-cannon replaced with 1 Kataphron plasma culverin.
- Any number of models can each have their phosphor blaster replaced with 1 cognis flamer.

ABILITIES

Canticles of the Omnissiah (pg 84-85)

Heavy Battle Servitor: Models in this unit do not suffer the penalty to hit rolls incurred for firing Heavy weapons in the same turn that their unit has moved.

Tracked Mobility: Models in this unit can move through the walls, girders, chains and foliage of terrain features with the Breachable terrain trait (see the Warhammer 40,000 Core Book) without impediment.

Bionics: Models in this unit have a 6+ invulnerable save.

FACTION KEYWORDS: IMPERIUM, ADEPTUS MECHANICUS, CULT MECHANICUS, <FORGE WORLD>
KEYWORDS: BIKER, KATAPHRON SERVITORS, KATAPHRON DESTROYERS

These biomechanical constructs operate as mobile heavy weapons platforms, bearing large esoteric cannon as well as close defence armaments. Their ballistic subroutines can be directed to operate independently of preprogrammed battle protocols, making them flexible tools of destruction.

Kataphron Destroyer with heavy grav-cannon and phosphor blaster

Kataphron Destroyer with Kataphron plasma culverin and cognis flamer

SERVITORS

No.	Name	M	WS	BS	S	T	W	A	Ld	Sv
4	Servitor	5"	5+	5+	3	3	1	1	6	4+

Every model is equipped with: servo-arm.

WEAPON	RANGE	TYPE	S	AP	D	ABILITIES
Heavy bolter	36"	Heavy 3	5	-1	2	-
Multi-melta	24"	Heavy 2	8	-4	D6	Each time an attack made with this weapon targets a unit within half range, that attack has a Damage characteristic of D6+2.
Plasma cannon		Before selecting targets, select one of the profiles below to make attacks with.				
- Standard	36"	Heavy D3	7	-3	1	Blast
- Supercharge	36"	Heavy D3	8	-3	2	Blast. If any unmodified hit rolls of 1 are made for attacks with this weapon profile, the bearer is destroyed after shooting with this weapon.
Servo-arm	Melee	Melee	x2	-2	3	Each time the bearer fights, no more than one attack can be made with each servo-arm.

WARGEAR OPTIONS

- Up to 2 models can each have their servo-arm replaced with one of the following: 1 heavy bolter; 1 multi-melta; 1 plasma cannon.

ABILITIES

Canticles of the Omnissiah (pg 84-85)

Bionics: Models in this unit have a 6+ invulnerable save.

Mindlock: While this unit is within 6" of any friendly <Forge World> Tech-Priest units, models in this unit have a Weapon Skill and Ballistic Skill characteristic of 4+ and a Leadership characteristic of 9. In addition, if your army is Battle-forged, then for each <Forge World> Tech-Priest unit included in a Detachment, one <Forge World> Servitors unit can be included in that Detachment without taking up a Battlefield Role slot.

FACTION KEYWORDS: Imperium, Adeptus Mechanicus, Cult Mechanicus, <Forge World>
KEYWORDS: Infantry, Servitors

Ubiquitous throughout the Imperium, mindless Servitors also accompany their priestly masters to war and aid them in heavy-duty technical endeavours. Protected by industrial cybernetics, their huge servo arms make for brutal weapons, while some are implanted with ranged weaponry with which they defend their creators' holy work.

Despite sinister rumours, no records have yet come to light of a devotee of the Machine God making a permanent transition to an entirely mechanical existence. While some aged Tech-Priests are little more than nervous systems operating mechanical bodies, most Tech-Priests and their cybernetic thralls retain portions of their flesh.

What is left, however, is grimy with oil and spattered with various fluids. Where skin remains, it is usually pale and sickly, resulting from their toil in the bowels of dark forge temples. They may employ rejuvenat processes on their remaining biological portions, but the arcane procedures eventually take their toll. Some resort to vat-grown replacements or take 'donations' from their underlings. Electro-Priests have a similarly wan complexion, scarified and puckered. When they activate their electoos, however, they positively shine. Those with poorly bonded electoos may smoke where the nodes break the surface of their skin, while others radiate with a variety of colours.

Once augmented, it is rare for Skitarii to ever remove their armour. Allied Guardsmen have sometimes witnessed severely damaged Skitarii with fractured helmets and witnessed what lies beneath: pallid and wrinkled flesh, sutured with bionics and with their eyelids cut away, while valves and sockets stud hard knots of muscle. Skitarii blessed with service as radium gunners have missing teeth and hairless, sore-pocked skin that tell the truth of their armour's theoretical protection against their wargear.

In the view of the Tech-Priests, servitors rank much lower than the Skitarii. They are disposable tools, sent into reactor cores, furnace grates and other inhospitable environments. Once lobotomised and fitted with the most rudimentary of bionics, their flesh quickly deteriorates. Only in exceptional circumstances would anything be done about it. Whether expected to survive a day or a month, there is an endless cycle of replacement servitors.

FULGURITE ELECTRO-PRIESTS

3 POWER

No.	Name	M	WS	BS	S	T	W	A	Ld	Sv
5-20	Fulgurite Electro-Priest	6"	3+	4+	3	3	1	2	8	6+

If this unit contains between 6 and 10 models, it has **Power Rating 6**. If this unit contains between 11 and 15 models, it has **Power Rating 9**. If this unit contains 16 or more models, it has **Power Rating 12**. Every model is equipped with: electroleech stave.

WEAPON	RANGE	TYPE	S	AP	D	ABILITIES
Electroleech stave	Melee	Melee	+2	-2	2	Each time an attack is made with this weapon, an unmodified wound roll of 6 inflicts 2 mortal wounds on the target and the attack sequence ends.

ABILITIES

Canticles of the Omnissiah (pg 84-85)

Voltagheist Field: Models in this unit have a 5+ invulnerable save.

Voltagheist Blast: After this unit finishes a charge move, select one enemy unit within Engagement Range of this unit and roll one D6 for each model from this unit that is within Engagement Range of that enemy unit: for each 6+, that enemy unit suffers 1 mortal wound.

Fanatical Devotion: Each time a model in this unit would lose a wound, roll one D6: on a 5+, that wound is not lost.

Siphoned Vigour: When this unit destroys an enemy unit for the first time, until the end of the battle:

- Add 1 to rolls made for this unit's Voltagheist Blast ability.
- Models in this unit have a 4+ invulnerable save.

FACTION KEYWORDS: IMPERIUM, ADEPTUS MECHANICUS, CULT MECHANICUS, <FORGE WORLD>
KEYWORDS: INFANTRY, CORE, ELECTRO-PRIESTS, FULGURITE ELECTRO-PRIESTS

Crackling with power stolen from those they slay, Fulgurite Electro-Priests are fanatical cultists of the Machine God. With their heavy, copper-bound staves, they smite blasphemers that waste the Motive Force, leeching it from heretic warriors and harnessing the holy energy in their capacitors where it empowers their voltagheist field.

CORPUSCARII ELECTRO-PRIESTS

3 POWER

No.	Name	M	WS	BS	S	T	W	A	Ld	Sv
5-20	Corpuscarii Electro-Priest	6"	4+	3+	3	3	1	2	8	6+

If this unit contains between 6 and 10 models, it has **Power Rating 6**. If this unit contains between 11 and 15 models, it has **Power Rating 9**. If this unit contains 16 or more models, it has **Power Rating 12**. Every model is equipped with: electrostatic gauntlets.

WEAPON	RANGE	TYPE	S	AP	D	ABILITIES
Electrostatic gauntlets (shooting)	12"	Assault 3	5	-1	1	Each time an attack is made with this weapon, an unmodified hit roll of 6 scores 2 additional hits.
Electrostatic gauntlets (melee)	Melee	Melee	+2	-1	1	Each time an attack is made with this weapon, an unmodified hit roll of 6 scores 2 additional hits.

ABILITIES

Canticles of the Omnissiah (pg 84-85)

Voltagheist Field: Models in this unit have a 5+ invulnerable save.

Voltagheist Blast: After this unit finishes a charge move, select one enemy unit within Engagement Range of this unit and roll one D6 for each model from this unit that is within Engagement Range of that enemy unit: for each 6+, that enemy unit suffers 1 mortal wound.

Fanatical Devotion: Each time a model in this unit would lose a wound, roll one D6: on a 5+, that wound is not lost.

Motive Force Sight: Each time a model in this unit makes a ranged attack, you can ignore any or all hit roll and Ballistic Skill modifiers.

FACTION KEYWORDS: IMPERIUM, ADEPTUS MECHANICUS, CULT MECHANICUS, <FORGE WORLD>
KEYWORDS: INFANTRY, CORE, ELECTRO-PRIESTS, CORPUSCARII ELECTRO-PRIESTS

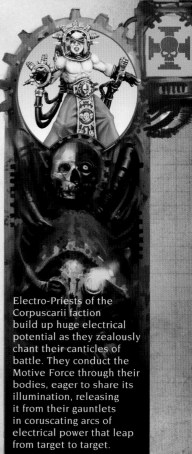

Electro-Priests of the Corpuscarii faction build up huge electrical potential as they zealously chant their canticles of battle. They conduct the Motive Force through their bodies, eager to share its illumination, releasing it from their gauntlets in coruscating arcs of electrical power that leap from target to target.

CYBERNETICA DATASMITH

2 POWER

No.	Name	M	WS	BS	S	T	W	A	Ld	Sv
1	Cybernetica Datasmith	6"	3+	3+	4	4	4	2	8	2+

A Cybernetica Datasmith is equipped with: gamma pistol; power fist.

WEAPON	RANGE	TYPE	S	AP	D	ABILITIES
Gamma pistol	12"	Pistol 1	6	-3	3	-
Power fist	Melee	Melee	x2	-3	2	Each time an attack is made with this weapon, subtract 1 from that attack's hit roll.

ABILITIES

Canticles of the Omnissiah (pg 84-85)

Refractor Field: This model has a 5+ invulnerable save.

Master of Machines: At the end of your Movement phase, this model can repair one friendly **<Forge World> Kastelan Robot** model within 3" of it. That **Kastelan Robot** model regains up to D3 lost wounds. Each model can only be repaired once per turn.

Battle Codifier: If your army is Battle-forged, then for each **Kastelan Robots** unit included in a Detachment, a **Cybernetica Datasmith** unit can be included in that Detachment without taking up an additional Battlefield Role slot.

Reprogramming: This model can attempt the following action:

'Field Reprogramming (Action): At the end of your Movement phase, any number of **Cybernetica Datasmith** models from your army can start to perform this action. When the action is started, select one friendly **<Forge World> Kastelan Robots** unit within 6" of the model performing the action and one of the available protocols found on that unit's datasheet. The action is completed at the end of your next Command phase. When it is completed, the selected protocol replaces that unit's active protocol.'

Machine Sentience (Aura): While a friendly **<Forge World> Kastelan Robots** unit is within 3" of this model, that unit gains the **Core** keyword.

FACTION KEYWORDS: **Imperium, Adeptus Mechanicus, Cult Mechanicus, <Forge World>**
KEYWORDS: **Infantry, Character, Doctrina Assembler, Tech-Priest, Cybernetica Datasmith**

Datasmiths optimise the programming of their robotic charges. These Tech-Priests employ rituals and binharic hymns to bless the doctrina wafers through which they alter the robots' protocols, all the while laying waste to the enemies of the Omnissiah with blasts of ionizing radiation from their gamma pistols.

SICARIAN INFILTRATORS

4 POWER

No.	Name	M	WS	BS	S	T	W	A	Ld	Sv
4-9	Sicarian Infiltrator	8"	3+	3+	4	3	2	2	6	4+
1	Sicarian Infiltrator Princeps	8"	3+	3+	4	3	2	3	7	4+

If this unit contains 6 or more models, it has **Power Rating 8**. Every model is equipped with: stubcarbine; power sword.

WEAPON	RANGE	TYPE	S	AP	D	ABILITIES
Flechette blaster	12"	Pistol 5	3	0	1	-
Stubcarbine	18"	Pistol 3	4	0	1	-
Power sword	Melee	Melee	+1	-3	1	-
Taser goad	Melee	Melee	+2	-1	1	Each time an attack is made with this weapon, an unmodified hit roll of 6 scores 2 additional hits.

WARGEAR OPTIONS

- Any number of models can each have their stubcarbine and power sword replaced with 1 flechette blaster and 1 taser goad.

ABILITIES

Doctrina Imperatives (see pg 85)

Enhanced Bionics: Models in this unit have a 5+ invulnerable save.

Neurostatic Interference: Each time an attack is made against this unit, if the attacking model is within 12", the hit roll cannot be re-rolled and the wound roll cannot be re-rolled.

Infiltrating Positions: During deployment, when you set up this unit, it can be set up anywhere on the battlefield that is more than 9" away from the enemy deployment zone and any enemy models.

Voices In The Code (Aura): While an enemy unit is within 3" of this unit, subtract 1 from the Leadership characteristic of models in that enemy unit.

FACTION KEYWORDS: **Imperium, Adeptus Mechanicus, Skitarii, <Forge World>**
KEYWORDS: **Infantry, Core, Sicarian, Sicarian Infiltrators**

Sicarian Infiltrators broadcast disruptive frequencies that scramble augurs and painfully disrupt enemy senses. Thus obscured, the Infiltrators perform reconnaissance and outflanking missions, intensifying their sensory barrage to crash enemy comms and attack unseen through the resultant anarchy.

SICARIAN RUSTSTALKERS

4 POWER

No.	Name	M	WS	BS	S	T	W	A	Ld	Sv
4-9	Sicarian Ruststalker	8"	3+	3+	4	3	2	3	6	4+
1	Sicarian Ruststalker Princeps	8"	3+	3+	4	3	2	4	7	4+

If this unit contains 6 or more models, it has **Power Rating 8**. Every model is equipped with: chordclaw; transonic razor.

WEAPON	RANGE	TYPE	S	AP	D	ABILITIES
Chordclaw	Melee	Melee	User	-1	1	Each time the bearer fights, it makes 1 additional attack with this weapon.
Transonic blades	Melee	Melee	+1	-3	1	Each time an attack is made with this weapon, an unmodified wound roll of 6 inflicts 1 mortal wound on the target in addition to any normal damage.
Transonic razor	Melee	Melee	User	-2	1	Each time an attack is made with this weapon, an unmodified wound roll of 6 inflicts 1 mortal wound on the target in addition to any normal damage.

WARGEAR OPTIONS

- Any number of Sicarian Ruststalkers can each have their chordclaw and transonic razer replaced with 1 transonic blades.
- The Sicarian Ruststalker Princeps' transonic razor can be replaced with 1 transonic blades.

ABILITIES

Doctrina Imperatives (see pg 85)

Optimised Gait: This unit can ignore any or all modifiers to its Move characteristic, with the exception of that incurred due to the Deprecation effect of the Bulwark Imperative (pg 85). This unit can ignore any or all modifiers to its Advance rolls and charge rolls.

Enhanced Bionics: Models in this unit have a 5+ invulnerable save.

Wasteland Stalkers: Each time a ranged attack is allocated to a model in this unit while it is receiving the benefits of cover, add an additional 1 to any armour saving throw made against that attack.

FACTION KEYWORDS: Imperium, Adeptus Mechanicus, Skitarii, <Forge World>
KEYWORDS: Infantry, Core, Sicarian, Sicarian Ruststalkers

Ruststalkers are unleashed as weapons of fear, to hunt down errant servo units and heretic blasphemers, or to pounce on isolated hostile units and assassinate enemy leaders. Like their fellow Sicarians, Ruststalkers' stilt-like limbs enable them to run down their prey swiftly, before carving their quarry apart with micro-vibrating transonic blades.

SERBERYS RAIDERS

No.	Name	M	WS	BS	S	T	W	A	Ld	Sv
2-8	Serberys Raider	12"	4+	3+	3	4	2	2	6	4+
1	Serberys Raider Alpha	12"	4+	3+	3	4	2	3	7	4+

If this unit contains between 4 and 6 models, it has **Power Rating 4**. If this unit contains 7 or more models, it has **Power Rating 6**.

- Every Serberys Raider is equipped with: galvanic carbine; cavalry sabre; clawed limbs.
- The Serberys Raider Alpha is equipped with: archeo-revolver; galvanic carbine; cavalry sabre; clawed limbs.

WEAPON	RANGE	TYPE	S	AP	D	ABILITIES
Archeo-revolver	12"	Pistol 1	5	-2	2	-
Galvanic carbine	18"	Assault 2	4	-1	1	-
Cavalry sabre	Melee	Melee	+1	-1	1	-
Clawed limbs	Melee	Melee	+1	0	1	Each time the bearer fights, it makes 2 additional attacks with this weapon.

OTHER WARGEAR	ABILITIES
Enhanced data-tether	While the bearer is on the battlefield: • The bearer's unit gains the **Data-Tether** keyword. • Add 1 to the Leadership characteristic of models in the bearer's unit.

WARGEAR OPTIONS

- 1 Serberys Raider can be equipped with 1 enhanced data-tether.

ABILITIES

Doctrina Imperatives (see pg 85)

Enhanced Bionics: Models in this unit have a 5+ invulnerable save.

Skirmishing Line: At the start of the first battle round, models in this unit can make a Normal Move. They cannot end this move within 9" of any enemy models.

Eye of Serberys: Each time you select a target for a weapon a model in this unit is equipped with, you can ignore the Look Out, Sir rule. Each time a ranged attack is made by a model in this unit, an unmodified wound roll of 6 inflicts 1 mortal wound on the target in addition to any normal damage.

FACTION KEYWORDS: Imperium, Adeptus Mechanicus, Skitarii, <Forge World>
KEYWORDS: Cavalry, Core, Serberys, Serberys Raiders

Long-range scouts and outriders, Raiders of the Serberys Corps employ advanced suites of sensors within their cybercanid mounts to identify enemy interlopers. They maintain punishing rates of carbine fire while moving at high speed, and when their prey can run no more, Raiders draw their sabres and charge into the fray.

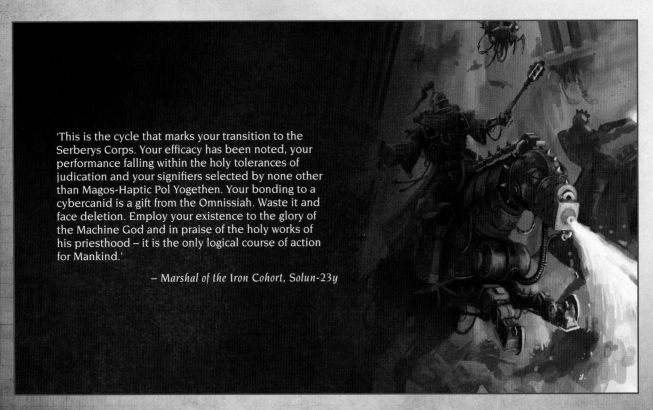

'This is the cycle that marks your transition to the Serberys Corps. Your efficacy has been noted, your performance falling within the holy tolerances of judication and your signifiers selected by none other than Magos-Haptic Pol Yogethen. Your bonding to a cybercanid is a gift from the Omnissiah. Waste it and face deletion. Employ your existence to the glory of the Machine God and in praise of the holy works of his priesthood – it is the only logical course of action for Mankind.'

– *Marshal of the Iron Cohort, Solun-23y*

SERBERYS SULPHURHOUNDS

3 POWER

No.	Name	M	WS	BS	S	T	W	A	Ld	Sv
2-8	Serberys Sulphurhound	12"	4+	3+	3	4	2	2	6	4+
1	Serberys Sulphurhound Alpha	12"	4+	3+	3	4	2	3	7	4+

If this unit contains between 4 and 6 models, it has **Power Rating 6**. If this unit contains 7 or more models, it has **Power Rating 9**.

- Every Serberys Sulphurhound is equipped with: 2 phosphor pistols; sulphur breath; clawed limbs.
- The Serberys Sulphurhound Alpha is equipped with: phosphor blast pistol; sulphur breath; arc maul; clawed limbs.

WEAPON	RANGE	TYPE	S	AP	D	ABILITIES
Phosphor blast carbine	18"	Assault 2D3	5	-1	1	Blast. Each time an attack is made with this weapon, the target does not receive the benefits of Dense Cover against that attack.
Phosphor blast pistol	12"	Pistol D3	5	-1	1	Blast. Each time an attack is made with this weapon, the target does not receive the benefits of Dense Cover against that attack.
Phosphor pistol	12"	Pistol 1	4	-1	1	Each time an attack is made with this weapon, the target does not receive the benefits of Dense Cover against that attack.
Sulphur breath	12"	Pistol D6	4	-2	1	Each time an attack is made with this weapon, that attack automatically hits the target.
Arc maul	Melee	Melee	+3	-2	1	Each time an attack is made with this weapon against a Vehicle unit, that attack has a Damage characteristic of 2 and an unmodified wound roll of 4+ successfully wounds the target.
Clawed limbs	Melee	Melee	+1	0	1	Each time the bearer fights, it makes 2 additional attacks with this weapon.

WARGEAR OPTIONS

- For every 3 models in this unit, 1 Serberys Sulphurhound's 2 phosphor pistols can be replaced with 1 phosphor blast carbine and 1 phosphor pistol.

ABILITIES

Doctrina Imperatives (see pg 85)

Pistoleers: Each time this unit Advances, until the end of the turn, the Type characteristic of Pistol weapons models in this unit are equipped with is changed to Assault. Models in this unit are eligible to shoot with any Assault weapons they are equipped with in a turn in which they shot Pistol weapons.

Enhanced Bionics: Models in this unit have a 5+ invulnerable save.

Rad-saturation (Aura): While an enemy unit (excluding **VEHICLE** units) is within Engagement Range of this unit, subtract 1 from the Strength and Toughness characteristics of models in that enemy unit.

FACTION KEYWORDS: IMPERIUM, ADEPTUS MECHANICUS, SKITARII, <FORGE WORLD>
KEYWORDS: CAVALRY, CORE, SERBERYS, SERBERYS SULPHURHOUNDS

Sulphurhound cavalry squadrons are aggressive shock troops and line-breakers. The loping, mechanical beasts breathe gouts of incinerating phosphor and disembowel the foe with slashing claws, while the elite Skitarii riders unload incandescent pistol fire as they smash through defence lines, before circling back for survivors.

PTERAXII STERYLIZORS

4 POWER

No.	Name	M	WS	BS	S	T	W	A	Ld	Sv
4-9	Pteraxii Sterylizor	12"	3+	3+	4	3	2	2	6	4+
1	Pteraxii Sterylizor Alpha	12"	3+	3+	4	3	2	3	7	4+

If this unit contains 6 or more models, it has **Power Rating 8**.
- Every Pteraxii Sterylizor is equipped with: phosphor torch; Pteraxii talons.
- The Pteraxii Sterylizor Alpha is equipped with: flechette blaster; Pteraxii talons; taser goad.

WEAPON	RANGE	TYPE	S	AP	D	ABILITIES
Flechette blaster	12"	Pistol 5	3	0	1	-
Phosphor torch	12"	Assault D6	4	-1	1	Each time an attack is made with this weapon, that attack automatically hits the target.
Pteraxii talons	Melee	Melee	User	-1	1	-
Taser goad	Melee	Melee	+2	-1	1	Each time an attack is made with this weapon, an unmodified hit roll of 6 scores 2 additional hits.

ABILITIES

Doctrina Imperatives (see pg 85)

Thermal Riders: During deployment, you can set up this unit high in the skies instead of setting it up on the battlefield. If you do so, then in the Reinforcements step of one of your Movement phases, you can set up this unit anywhere on the battlefield that is more than 9" away from any enemy models.

Enhanced Bionics: Models in this unit have a 5+ invulnerable save.

Darting Hunters: This unit is eligible to charge in a turn in which it Fell Back.

Swooping Strikes: Each time this unit fights, if it made a charge move or was charged, then until that fight is resolved, add 1 to the Attacks characteristic of models in this unit.

FACTION KEYWORDS: IMPERIUM, ADEPTUS MECHANICUS, SKITARII, <FORGE WORLD>
KEYWORDS: INFANTRY, JUMP PACK, FLY, CORE, PTERAXII, PTERAXII STERYLIZORS

Sterylizors are eradicators of cybernetic parasite organisms within ships and manufactora, and eagerly unleash the chemical fire of their phosphor torches upon the Machine God's foes. They descend in flocks from the sky upon membranous wing-packs, their vicious talons primed, eager to see their enemies writhe in flames.

PTERAXII SKYSTALKERS

4 POWER

No.	Name	M	WS	BS	S	T	W	A	Ld	Sv
4-9	Pteraxii Skystalker	12"	3+	3+	4	3	2	2	6	4+
1	Pteraxii Skystalker Alpha	12"	3+	3+	4	3	2	3	7	4+

If this unit contains 6 or more models, it has **Power Rating 8**.
- Every Pteraxii Skystalker is equipped with: flechette carbine.
- The Pteraxii Skystalker Alpha is equipped with: flechette blaster; taser goad.

WEAPON	RANGE	TYPE	S	AP	D	ABILITIES
Flechette blaster	12"	Pistol 5	3	0	1	-
Flechette carbine	18"	Assault 5	3	0	1	-
Taser goad	Melee	Melee	+2	-1	1	Each time an attack is made with this weapon, an unmodified hit roll of 6 scores 2 additional hits.

ABILITIES

Doctrina Imperatives (see pg 85)

Enhanced Bionics: Models in this unit have a 5+ invulnerable save.

Fleeting Barrage: This unit is eligible to shoot in a turn in which it Fell Back.

Thermal Riders: During deployment, you can set up this unit high in the skies instead of setting it up on the battlefield. If you do so, then in the Reinforcements step of one of your Movement phases you can set up this unit anywhere on the battlefield that is more than 9" away from any enemy models.

FACTION KEYWORDS: IMPERIUM, ADEPTUS MECHANICUS, SKITARII, <FORGE WORLD>
KEYWORDS: INFANTRY, JUMP PACK, FLY, CORE, PTERAXII, ARC GRENADES, PTERAXII SKYSTALKERS

Pteraxii Skystalkers have their consciousness pared back until little but their optimized reactions remain. They are manoeuvrable and preternatural airborne hunters, who track their prey from choice vantage points before swooping in to unleash withering hails of razor-sharp flechettes.

IRONSTRIDER BALLISTARII

4 POWER

No.	Name	M	WS	BS	S	T	W	A	Ld	Sv
1-6	Ironstrider Ballistarii	10"	3+	3+	5	6	6	2	8	3+

Increase this unit's **Power Rating** by **+4** for every additional Ironstrider Ballistarii it includes. Every model is equipped with: twin cognis autocannon.

WEAPON	RANGE	TYPE	S	AP	D	ABILITIES
Twin cognis autocannon	48"	Assault 6	7	-1	2	-
Twin cognis lascannon	48"	Assault 2	9	-3	D3+3	-

WARGEAR OPTIONS

- Any number of models can each have their twin cognis autocannon replaced with 1 twin cognis lascannon.

ABILITIES

Doctrina Imperatives (see pg 85)

Bionics: Models in this unit have a 6+ invulnerable save.

Explodes: Each time a model in this unit is destroyed, roll one D6 before removing it from play. On a 6 it explodes, and each unit within 3" suffers 1 mortal wound.

Broad Spectrum Data-tether: In your Command phase, select one friendly <FORGE WORLD> SKITARII CORE unit within 6" of this unit. Until the start of your next Command phase, add 1 to the Leadership characteristic of models in that unit and that unit gains the **DATA-TETHER** keyword.

FACTION KEYWORDS: IMPERIUM, ADEPTUS MECHANICUS, SKITARII, <FORGE WORLD>
KEYWORDS: VEHICLE, CORE, DATA-TETHER, IRONSTRIDER ENGINE, IRONSTRIDER BALLISTARII

Ironstrider Ballistarii are swift combat walkers piloted by veteran marksmen. They smoothly pick their way across the battlefield before invoking the fully awakened machine spirits of their weapons to acquire rapidly cogitated firing solutions. Their destructive firepower unleashed, they redeploy to hunt for fresh targets.

SYDONIAN DRAGOONS

4 POWER

No.	Name	M	WS	BS	S	T	W	A	Ld	Sv
1-6	Sydonian Dragoon	10"	3+	3+	5	6	6	4	8	3+

Increase this unit's **Power Rating** by **+4** for every additional Sydonian Dragoon it includes. Every model is equipped with: radium jezzail.

WEAPON	RANGE	TYPE	S	AP	D	ABILITIES
Phosphor serpenta	18"	Assault 1	5	-1	1	Each time an attack is made with this weapon, the target does not receive the benefits of Dense Cover against that attack.
Radium jezzail	30"	Heavy 2	5	-2	1	Each time you select a target for this weapon, you can ignore the Look Out, Sir rule. Each time an attack is made with this weapon against an enemy unit (excluding **Vehicle** units), an unmodified hit roll of 6 automatically wounds the target.
Taser lance	Melee	Melee	+3	-2	2	Each time an attack is made with this weapon, an unmodified hit roll of 6 scores 2 additional hits.

WARGEAR OPTIONS

- Any number of models can each have their radium jezzail replaced with 1 taser lance.
- Any number of models can each be equipped with 1 phosphor serpenta.

ABILITIES

Doctrina Imperatives (see pg 85)

Bionics: Models in this unit have a 6+ invulnerable save.

Explodes: Each time a model in this unit is destroyed, roll one D6 before removing it from play. On a 6 it explodes, and each unit within 3" suffers 1 mortal wound.

Incense Cloud: Each time an attack is made against this unit, subtract 1 from that attack's hit roll.

Broad Spectrum Data-tether: In your Command phase, select one friendly <**Forge World**> **Skitarii Core** unit within 6" of this unit. Until the start of your next Command phase, add 1 to the Leadership characteristic of models in that unit and that unit gains the **Data-tether** keyword.

FACTION KEYWORDS: Imperium, Adeptus Mechanicus, Skitarii, <Forge World>
KEYWORDS: Vehicle, Core, Data-tether, Ironstrider Engine, Sydonian Dragoons

Striding through a mist of their own sacred incense, the long-limbed engines ridden by Sydonian Dragoons are forever in motion. Dragoons mark their quarry with shots of glowing phosphor or irradiated slugs, allowing them to detect their prey through the cloying mist, and to home in on with a thunderous stampede.

KASTELAN ROBOTS

10 POWER

No.	Name	M	WS	BS	S	T	W	A	Ld	Sv
2-6	Kastelan Robot	8"	4+	4+	6	7	7	3	10	3+

If this unit contains between 3 and 4 models, it has **Power Rating 20**. If this unit contains between 5 and 6 models, it has **Power Rating 30**. Every model is equipped with: Kastelan phosphor blaster; incendine combustor; Kastelan fist.

WEAPON	RANGE	TYPE	S	AP	D	ABILITIES
Heavy phosphor blaster	36"	Heavy 3	6	-2	1	Each time an attack is made with this weapon, the target does not receive the benefits of Dense Cover against that attack.
Incendine combustor	12"	Heavy D6	5	-2	1	Each time an attack is made with this weapon, that attack automatically hits the target.
Kastelan phosphor blaster	24"	Heavy 3	6	-1	2	Each time an attack is made with this weapon, the target does not receive the benefits of Dense Cover against that attack.
Kastelan fist	Melee	Melee	+4	-3	3	Each time the bearer fights, it makes 1 additional attack with this weapon.

WARGEAR OPTIONS

- Any number of models can each have their Kastelan fist replaced with 1 Kastelan phosphor blaster.
- Any number of models can each have their Kastelan phosphor blaster replaced with 1 Kastelan fist.
- Any number of models can each have their incendine combustor replaced with 1 heavy phosphor blaster.

ABILITIES

Canticles of the Omnissiah (pg 84-85)

Battle Protocols: This unit receives a bonus depending on which protocol is active for it. At the start of the battle, the Aegis Protocol (see below) is active for this unit. To change the unit's active protocol see the Cybernetica Datasmith datasheet (pg 98). The available protocols are:

- **Aegis Protocol:** While this protocol is active for this unit, models in this unit have a Sv characteristic of 2+.

- **Conqueror Protocol:** While this protocol is active for this unit, you can re-roll charge rolls made for it and models in this unit have a WS characteristic of 2+.

- **Protector Protocol:** While this protocol is active for this unit, it cannot move (except to pile in or consolidate) and models in this unit have a BS characteristic of 3+.

Repulsor Grid: Models in this unit have a 5+ invulnerable save against ranged attacks. Each time an invulnerable saving throw is made for a model in this unit against a ranged attack, on an unmodified saving roll of 6, the attacking model's unit suffers 1 mortal wound.

Explodes: Each time a model in this unit is destroyed, roll one D6 before removing it from play. On a 6 it explodes, and each unit within 3" suffers 1 mortal wound.

FACTION KEYWORDS: IMPERIUM, ADEPTUS MECHANICUS, CULT MECHANICUS, <FORGE WORLD>

KEYWORDS: VEHICLE, KASTELAN ROBOTS

Kastelan Robots are giant automata from Mankind's dark past, shielded with thick armour and advanced force fields. Heeding preprogrammed doctrines without fail, Kastelans are bastions in defence and nigh unstoppable on the attack, unleashing heavy firepower and bludgeoning swipes with their giant fists.

SKORPIUS DISINTEGRATOR

Some of this model's characteristics change as it suffers damage, as shown below:

No.	Name	M	WS	BS	S	T	W	A	Ld	Sv
1	Skorpius Disintegrator (7+ wounds remaining)	12"	6+	3+	6	7	12	3	8	3+
	Skorpius Disintegrator (4-6 wounds remaining)	9"	6+	4+	6	7	N/A	D3	8	3+
	Skorpius Disintegrator (1-3 wounds remaining)	6"	6+	5+	6	7	N/A	1	8	3+

A Skorpius Disintegrator is equipped with: 3 cognis heavy stubbers; disruptor missile launcher; belleros energy cannon.

WEAPON	RANGE	TYPE	S	AP	D	ABILITIES
Belleros energy cannon	36"	Heavy 3D3	5	-1	2	Blast. This weapon can target units that are not visible to the bearer.
Cognis heavy stubber	36"	Assault 4	4	0	1	-
Disruptor missile launcher	36"	Heavy D6	7	-2	D3	Blast
Ferrumite cannon	48"	Heavy 3	8	-3	3	-

WARGEAR OPTIONS

• This model's belleros energy cannon can be replaced with 1 ferrumite cannon.

ABILITIES

Doctrina Imperatives (see pg 85)

Explodes: When this model is destroyed, roll one D6 before removing it from play. On a 6 it explodes, and each unit within 6" suffers D3 mortal wounds.

Broad Spectrum Data-tether: In your Command phase, select one friendly <Forge World> Skitarii Core unit within 6" of this model. Until the start of your next Command phase, add 1 to the Leadership characteristic of models in that unit and that unit gains the Data-tether keyword.

FACTION KEYWORDS: **Imperium, Adeptus Mechanicus, Skitarii, <Forge World>**
KEYWORDS: **Vehicle, Data-tether, Skorpius Engine, Skorpius Disintegrator**

Hovering over the ruins of war on a bed of atomised gases, Skorpius Disintegrators are archaic, front-line battle tanks. They surge forward in unstoppable armoured waves and support infantry advances, maintaining blistering salvoes of fire to cripple enemy war engines and sweep aside hordes of lesser foes.

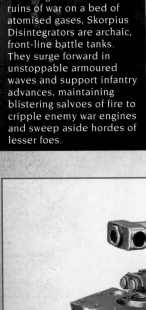

ONAGER DUNECRAWLER

6 POWER

Some of this model's characteristics change as it suffers damage, as shown below:

No.	Name	M	WS	BS	S	T	W	A	Ld	Sv
1	Onager Dunecrawler (6+ wounds remaining)	8"	5+	3+	6	7	11	3	8	3+
	Onager Dunecrawler (3-5 wounds remaining)	6"	5+	4+	6	7	N/A	D3	8	3+
	Onager Dunecrawler (1-2 wounds remaining)	4"	5+	5+	6	7	N/A	1	8	3+

An Onager Dunecrawler is equipped with: eradication beamer.

WEAPON	RANGE	TYPE	S	AP	D	ABILITIES
Cognis heavy stubber	36"	Assault 4	4	0	1	-
Daedalus missile launcher	48"	Heavy 1	7	-3	D6	Each time an attack is made with this weapon profile against an AIRCRAFT unit, add 1 to that attack's hit roll.
Eradication beamer		Before selecting targets, select one of the profiles below to make attacks with.				
- Focused	18"	Heavy D6	8	-4	3	Blast
- Dissipated	36"	Heavy D6	8	-3	2	Blast
Gatling rocket launcher	48"	Heavy 5	6	-2	1	Each time an attack is made with this weapon profile against an AIRCRAFT unit, add 1 to that attack's hit roll.
Neutron laser	48"	Heavy D3	12	-4	D3+3	Blast
Twin Icarus autocannon	48"	Heavy 4	7	-1	2	Each time an attack is made with this weapon profile against an AIRCRAFT unit, add 1 to that attack's hit roll.
Twin Onager heavy phosphor blaster	36"	Heavy 8	6	-2	2	Each time an attack is made with this weapon, the target does not receive the benefits of Dense Cover against that attack.

OTHER WARGEAR	ABILITIES
Broad spectrum data-tether	In your Command phase, select one friendly <FORGE WORLD> SKITARII CORE unit within 6" of the bearer. Until the start of your next Command phase, add 1 to the Leadership characteristic of models in that unit and that unit gains the DATA-TETHER keyword.
Smoke launchers	The bearer gains the SMOKESCREEN keyword.

WARGEAR OPTIONS

- This model's eradication beamer can be replaced with one of the following: 1 daedalus missile launcher, 1 gatling rocket launcher and 1 twin icarus autocannon; 1 neutron laser and 1 cognis heavy stubber; 1 twin Onager heavy phosphor blaster.
- This model can be equipped with 1 additional cognis heavy stubber.
- This model can be equipped with one of the following: broad spectrum data-tether; smoke launchers.

ABILITIES

Doctrina Imperatives (see pg 85)

Emanatus Force Field: This model has a 5+ invulnerable save.

Explodes: When this model is destroyed, roll one D6 before removing it from play. On a 6 it explodes, and each unit within 6" suffers D3 mortal wounds.

FACTION KEYWORDS: IMPERIUM, ADEPTUS MECHANICUS, SKITARII, <FORGE WORLD>
KEYWORDS: VEHICLE, ONAGER DUNECRAWLER

The Onager Dunecrawler's flexible armaments can blast apart squadrons of aircraft, punch through enemy tanks or atomise elite infantry in beams of blinding energy. They are versatile heavy weapons platforms, well-shielded and easily able to advance alongside Skitarii as their multiple limbs propel them over treacherous obstacles.

SKORPIUS DUNERIDER

Some of this model's characteristics change as it suffers damage, as shown below:

No.	Name	M	WS	BS	S	T	W	A	Ld	Sv
1	Skorpius Dunerider (7+ wounds remaining)	12"	6+	3+	6	6	12	3	8	3+
	Skorpius Dunerider (4-6 wounds remaining)	9"	6+	4+	6	6	N/A	D3	8	3+
	Skorpius Dunerider (1-3 wounds remaining)	6"	6+	5+	6	6	N/A	1	8	3+

A Skorpius Dunerider is equipped with: 2 cognis heavy stubbers; twin cognis heavy stubber.

WEAPON	RANGE	TYPE	S	AP	D	ABILITIES
Cognis heavy stubber	36"	Assault 4	4	0	1	-
Twin cognis heavy stubber	36"	Assault 8	4	0	1	-

ABILITIES

Doctrina Imperatives (see pg 85)

Explodes: When this transport is destroyed, roll one D6 before any embarked models disembark and before removing it from play. On a 6 it explodes, and each unit within 6" suffers D3 mortal wounds.

Broad Spectrum Data-tether: In your Command phase, select one friendly <FORGE WORLD> SKITARII CORE unit within 6" of this model. Until the start of your next Command phase, add 1 to the Leadership characteristic of models in that unit and that unit gains the DATA-TETHER keyword.

TRANSPORT

This model has a transport capacity of 12 INFANTRY or <FORGE WORLD> INFANTRY models.

FACTION KEYWORDS: IMPERIUM, ADEPTUS MECHANICUS, SKITARII, <FORGE WORLD>
KEYWORDS: VEHICLE, TRANSPORT, DATA-TETHER, SKORPIUS ENGINE, SKORPIUS DUNERIDER

Skorpius Duneriders enable forge lords to ferry squads of their cyborg infantry onto the front lines, overwhelming the foe through swiftly redeployed weight of numbers. Duneriders sweep onto enemy defences in a cloud of chemical smoke, saturating the area with heavy calibre shot as their payload of warriors disembarks.

ARCHAEOPTER TRANSVECTOR

6 POWER

Some of this model's characteristics change as it suffers damage, as shown below:

No.	Name	M	WS	BS	S	T	W	A	Ld	Sv
1	Archaeopter Transvector (6+ wounds remaining)	20-50"	5+	3+	6	7	10	3	9	3+
	Archaeopter Transvector (3-5 wounds remaining)	20-35"	5+	4+	6	7	N/A	D3	9	3+
	Archaeopter Transvector (1-2 wounds remaining)	20-25"	5+	5+	6	7	N/A	1	9	3+

An Archaeopter Transvector is equipped with: 2 cognis heavy stubbers; twin cognis heavy stubber; command uplink.

WEAPON	RANGE	TYPE	S	AP	D	ABILITIES
Cognis heavy stubber	36"	Assault 4	4	0	1	-
Twin cognis heavy stubber	36"	Assault 8	4	0	1	-

OTHER WARGEAR	ABILITIES
Chaff launcher	The bearer gains the **SMOKESCREEN** keyword. Each time an attack is allocated to the bearer, subtract 1 from the Damage characteristic of that attack (to a minimum of 1).
Command uplink	The bearer gains the **DATA-TETHER** keyword and the following ability: '**Command Uplink (Aura):** While a friendly <**FORGE WORLD**> **SKITARII CORE** unit is within 3" of this model, add 1 to the Leadership characteristic of models in that unit and that unit gains the **DATA-TETHER** keyword.

WARGEAR OPTIONS

- This model's command uplink can be replaced with 1 chaff launcher.

ABILITIES

Doctrina Imperatives (see pg 85)

Combined Landing: If a Detachment contains multiple **ARCHAEOPTER TRANSVECTOR** models, you can choose for pairs of them to make combined landings instead of setting them up on the battlefield. For each combined landing that you want to make, select two <**FORGE WORLD**> **ARCHAEOPTER TRANSVECTOR** models:

- Those two **TRANSPORT** models are treated as one model with a combined transport capacity of 12 <**FORGE WORLD**> **INFANTRY** models for the purpose of which units can be embarked within them. This means that an eligible **INFANTRY** unit containing 7-12 models can start the battle embarked within these two **TRANSPORT** models, the **INFANTRY** models in that unit being split between the two transports. Make a note of which **INFANTRY** models are embarked within which **TRANSPORT** models.

- Those two **TRANSPORT** models can be set up in the Reinforcements step of your first, second or third Movement phase, regardless of any mission rules, and must be set up at the same time. Any units embarked within those **TRANSPORT** models must immediately disembark after the **TRANSPORT** models have been set up, and the disembarking units must be set up more than 9" away from any enemy models.

- When those two **TRANSPORT** models are set up, they must be set up within 9" of one another, and any disembarking units must follow the normal rules for disembarking transports and unit coherency.

Hard to Hit: Each time a ranged attack is made against this model, subtract 1 from that attack's hit roll.

Hover Jet: In your Command phase, this model can hover. If it does so, then until the start of your next Command phase, its Move characteristic becomes 20" and it loses the Airborne, Hard to Hit and Manoeuvrable Craft abilities.

Aerial Deployment: If your army is Battle-forged, then for each **ARCHAEOPTER TRANSVECTOR** unit included in a Detachment, a second **ARCHAEOPTER TRANSVECTOR** unit can be included in that Detachment without taking up an additional Battlefield Role slot.

Explodes: When this transport is destroyed, roll one D6 before any embarked models disembark and before removing it from play. On a 6 it explodes, and each unit within 6" suffers D3 mortal wounds.

Airborne: You cannot declare a charge with this model, and it can only be chosen as a target of a charge if the unit making the charge can **FLY**. You can only fight with this model if it is within Engagement Range of any enemy units that can **FLY**, and this model can only make melee attacks against units that can **FLY**. Enemy units can only make melee attacks against this model if they can **FLY**.

Manoeuvrable Craft: Each time this model makes a Normal Move, Advances or Falls Back, first pivot it on the spot up to 90° (this does not contribute to how far the model moves), then move the model straight forwards. It can pivot up to 90° one more time, at any point, during the move.

TRANSPORT

This model has a transport capacity of 6 **INFANTRY** or <**FORGE WORLD**> **INFANTRY** models.

FACTION KEYWORDS: IMPERIUM, ADEPTUS MECHANICUS, SKITARII, <**FORGE WORLD**>

KEYWORDS: VEHICLE, AIRCRAFT, TRANSPORT, FLY, ARCHAEOPTER ENGINE, ARCHAEOPTER TRANSVECTOR

Ideal aerial insertion transports, Transvectors are used in vast numbers by Explorator fleets for reconnaissance and rapid extraction in the face of hostiles. They are incredibly agile, their implanted pilots able to reshape the wings to suit changing atmospherics, while directing their cognis heavy stubbers to scythe apart oncoming foes.

ARCHAEOPTER STRATORAPTOR

9 POWER

Some of this model's characteristics change as it suffers damage, as shown below:

No.	Name	M	WS	BS	S	T	W	A	Ld	Sv
1	Archaeopter Stratoraptor (6+ wounds remaining)	20-50"	5+	3+	6	7	10	3	9	3+
	Archaeopter Stratoraptor (3-5 wounds remaining)	20-35"	5+	4+	6	7	N/A	D3	9	3+
	Archaeopter Stratoraptor (1-2 wounds remaining)	20-25"	5+	5+	6	7	N/A	1	9	3+

An Archaeopter Stratoraptor is equipped with: 2 cognis heavy stubbers; 2 heavy phosphor blasters; twin cognis lascannon; command uplink.

WEAPON	RANGE	TYPE	S	AP	D	ABILITIES
Cognis heavy stubber	36"	Assault 4	4	0	1	-
Heavy phosphor blaster	36"	Heavy 3	6	-2	1	Each time an attack is made with this weapon, the target does not receive the benefits of Dense Cover against that attack.
Twin cognis lascannon	48"	Assault 2	9	-3	D3+3	-

OTHER WARGEAR	ABILITIES
Chaff launcher	The bearer gains the **SMOKESCREEN** keyword. Each time an attack is allocated to the bearer, subtract 1 from the Damage characteristic of that attack (to a minimum of 1).
Command uplink	The bearer gains the **DATA-TETHER** keyword and the following ability: '**Command Uplink (Aura):** While a friendly <FORGE WORLD> SKITARII CORE unit is within 3" of this model, add 1 to the Leadership characteristic of models in that unit and that unit gains the **DATA-TETHER** keyword.

WARGEAR OPTIONS

• This model's command uplink can be replaced with 1 chaff launcher.

ABILITIES

Doctrina Imperatives (see pg 85)

Airborne: You cannot declare a charge with this model, and it can only be chosen as a target of a charge if the unit making the charge can **FLY**. You can only fight with this model if it is within Engagement Range of any enemy units that can **FLY**, and this model can only make melee attacks against units that can **FLY**. Enemy units can only make melee attacks against this model if they can **FLY**.

Manoeuvrable Craft: Each time this model makes a Normal Move, Advances or Falls Back, first pivot it on the spot up to 90° (this does not contribute to how far the model moves), then move the model straight forwards. It can pivot up to 90° one more time, at any point, during the move.

Hard to Hit: Each time a ranged attack is made against this model, subtract 1 from that attack's hit roll.

Hover Jet: In your Command phase, this model can hover. If it does so, then until the start of your next Command phase, its Move characteristic becomes 20" and it loses the Airborne, Hard to Hit and Manoeuvrable Craft abilities.

Explodes: When this model is destroyed, roll one D6 before removing it from play. On a 6 it explodes, and each unit within 6" suffers D3 mortal wounds.

FACTION KEYWORDS: IMPERIUM, ADEPTUS MECHANICUS, SKITARII, <FORGE WORLD>
KEYWORDS: VEHICLE, AIRCRAFT, FLY, ARCHAEOPTER ENGINE, ARCHAEOPTER STRATORAPTOR

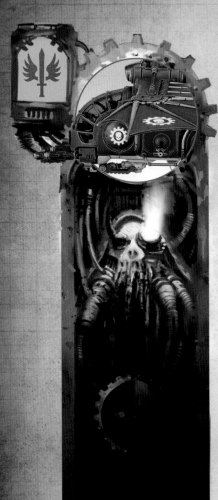

The Stratoraptor takes advantage of the Archaeopter's directional thrusters and adaptable wing profile to excel in the role of ground attack gunship. Its spread of heavy weapons – with a mixture of high strength and high rate of fire – ensures the Stratoraptor poses a lethal danger to dug-in infantry and heavily armoured vehicles alike.

ARCHAEOPTER FUSILAVE

7 POWER

Some of this model's characteristics change as it suffers damage, as shown below:

No.	Name	M	WS	BS	S	T	W	A	Ld	Sv
1	Archaeopter Fusilave (6+ wounds remaining)	20-50"	5+	3+	6	7	10	3	9	3+
	Archaeopter Fusilave (3-5 wounds remaining)	20-35"	5+	4+	6	7	N/A	D3	9	3+
	Archaeopter Fusilave (1-2 wounds remaining)	20-25"	5+	5+	6	7	N/A	1	9	3+

An Archaeopter Fusilave is equipped with: 4 cognis heavy stubbers; command uplink.

WEAPON	RANGE	TYPE	S	AP	D	ABILITIES
Cognis heavy stubber	36"	Assault 4	4	0	1	-

OTHER WARGEAR	ABILITIES
Chaff launcher	The bearer gains the **SMOKESCREEN** keyword. Each time an attack is allocated to the bearer, subtract 1 from the Damage characteristic of that attack (to a minimum of 1).
Command uplink	The bearer gains the **DATA-TETHER** keyword and the following ability: '**Command Uplink (Aura):** While a friendly **<FORGE WORLD> SKITARII CORE** unit is within 3" of this model, add 1 to the Leadership characteristic of models in that unit and that unit gains the **DATA-TETHER** keyword.

WARGEAR OPTIONS

• This model's command uplink can be replaced with 1 chaff launcher.

ABILITIES

Doctrina Imperatives (see pg 85)

Bomb Rack: Once per turn, after this model has moved in your Movement phase, you can select one unit it moved across. Roll six D6s for each **VEHICLE** or **MONSTER** model in that unit and roll one D6 for each other model in that unit (to a maximum of ten D6s): for each 4+, that unit suffers 1 mortal wound.

Airborne: You cannot declare a charge with this model, and it can only be chosen as a target of a charge if the unit making the charge can **FLY**. You can only fight with this model if it is within Engagement Range of any enemy units that can **FLY**, and this model can only make melee attacks against units that can **FLY**. Enemy units can only make melee attacks against this model if they can **FLY**.

Manoeuvrable Craft: Each time this model makes a Normal Move, Advances or Falls Back, first pivot it on the spot up to 90° (this does not contribute to how far the model moves), then move the model straight forwards. It can pivot up to 90° one more time, at any point, during the move.

Hard to Hit: Each time a ranged attack is made against this model, subtract 1 from that attack's hit roll.

Hover Jet: In your Command phase, this model can hover. If it does so, then until the start of your next Command phase, its Move characteristic becomes 20" and it loses the Airborne, Hard to Hit and Manoeuvrable Craft abilities.

Explodes: When this model is destroyed, roll one D6 before removing it from play. On a 6 it explodes, and each unit within 6" suffers D3 mortal wounds.

FACTION KEYWORDS: **IMPERIUM, ADEPTUS MECHANICUS, SKITARII, <FORGE WORLD>**

KEYWORDS: **VEHICLE, AIRCRAFT, FLY, ARCHAEOPTER ENGINE, ARCHAEOPTER FUSILAVE**

The Archaeopter Fusilave's changeable payload of deep-bore, high explosives defines its position as a devastating bomber and ground clearance aircraft. Tech-Priests employ whole squadrons to level enemy defences and root out sheltering heretics, as well as to clear prospective sites for further investigation in the Quest for Knowledge.

WEAPON PROFILES

Below you will find the profiles for all the weapons that Adeptus Mechanicus models can be equipped with. Note that some weapons have the Blast ability; this ability is detailed in full in the Warhammer 40,000 Core Book.

WEAPON DEFINITIONS

Some rules refer to 'arc weapons' or 'radium weapons' and so on. The definitions of these weapons for the purposes of such rules can be found below:

ARC WEAPONS

An arc weapon is any weapon whose profile includes the word 'arc' (arc claw, arc rifle, etc.), and any Relic that replaces such a weapon.

CARBINE WEAPONS

A carbine weapon is any ranged weapon whose profile includes the word 'carbine' (radium carbine, stubcarbine, etc.), and any Relic that replaces such a weapon.

COGNIS WEAPONS

A cognis weapon is any ranged weapon whose profile includes the word 'cognis' (cognis flamer, cognis heavy stubber, etc.), and any Relic that replaces such a weapon.

GALVANIC WEAPONS

A galvanic weapon is any ranged weapon whose profile includes the word 'galvanic' (galvanic carbine, galvanic rifle, etc.), and any Relic that replaces such a weapon.

PHOSPHOR WEAPONS

A phosphor weapon is any ranged weapon whose profile includes the word 'phosphor' (phosphor blaster, phosphor serpenta, etc.), and any Relic that replaces such a weapon.

PLASMA WEAPONS

A plasma weapon is any ranged weapon whose profile includes the word 'plasma' (plasma caliver, plasma cannon, etc.), and any Relic that replaces such a weapon.

RADIUM WEAPONS

A radium weapon is any ranged weapon whose profile includes the word 'radium' (radium carbine, radium pistol, etc.), and any Relic that replaces such a weapon.

RIFLE WEAPONS

A rifle weapon is any ranged weapon whose profile includes the word 'rifle' (arc rifle, galvanic rifle, etc.), and any Relic that replaces such a weapon.

TASER WEAPONS

A taser weapon is any melee weapon whose profile includes the word 'taser' (taser goad, taser lance, etc.), and any Relic that replaces such a weapon.

RANGED WEAPONS	RANGE	TYPE	S	AP	D	ABILITIES
Arc pistol	12"	Pistol 1	5	-2	1	Each time an attack is made with this weapon against a **Vehicle** unit, that attack has a Damage characteristic of 2 and an unmodified wound roll of 4+ successfully wounds the target.
Arc rifle	30"	Rapid Fire 1	6	-2	D3	Each time an attack is made with this weapon against a **Vehicle** unit, that attack has a Damage characteristic of 3 and an unmodified wound roll of 4+ successfully wounds the target.
Archeo-revolver	12"	Pistol 1	5	-2	2	-
Belleros energy cannon	36"	Heavy 3D3	5	-1	2	Blast. This weapon can target units that are not visible to the bearer.
Cognis flamer	12"	Assault D6+2	4	0	1	Each time an attack is made with this weapon, that attack automatically hits the target.
Cognis heavy stubber	36"	Assault 4	4	0	1	-
Daedalus missile launcher	48"	Heavy 1	7	-3	D6	Each time an attack is made with this weapon profile against an **Aircraft** unit, add 1 to that attack's hit roll.
Disruptor missile launcher	36"	Heavy D6	7	-2	D3	Blast
Electrostatic gauntlets (shooting)	12"	Assault 3	5	-1	1	Each time an attack is made with this weapon, an unmodified hit roll of 6 scores 2 additional hits.
Eradication beamer		Before selecting targets, select one of the profiles below to make attacks with.				
- Focused	18"	Heavy D6	8	-4	3	Blast
- Dissipated	36"	Heavy D6	8	-3	2	Blast
Eradication pistol		Before selecting targets, select one of the profiles below to make attacks with.				
- Focused	6"	Pistol D3	6	-3	2	Blast
- Dissipated	12"	Pistol D3	6	-2	1	Blast
Eradication ray		Before selecting targets, select one of the profiles below to make attacks with.				
- Focused	12"	Heavy D3	6	-3	2	Blast
- Dissipated	24"	Heavy D3	6	-2	1	Blast
Ferrumite cannon	48"	Heavy 3	8	-3	3	-
Flechette blaster	12"	Pistol 5	3	0	1	-
Flechette carbine	18"	Assault 5	3	0	1	-
Galvanic carbine	18"	Assault 2	4	-1	1	-
Galvanic rifle	30"	Heavy 2	4	-1	1	-
Gamma pistol	12"	Pistol 1	6	-3	3	-

RANGED WEAPONS	RANGE	TYPE	S	AP	D	ABILITIES
Gatling rocket launcher	48"	Heavy 5	6	-2	1	Each time an attack is made with this weapon profile against an **AIRCRAFT** unit, add 1 to that attack's hit roll.
Heavy arc rifle	36"	Heavy 2	6	-2	2	Each time an attack is made with this weapon against a **VEHICLE** unit, that attack has a Damage characteristic of 3 and an unmodified wound roll of 4+ successfully wounds the target.
Heavy bolter	36"	Heavy 3	5	-1	2	-
Heavy grav-cannon	30"	Heavy 5	5	-3	1	Each time an attack made with this weapon is allocated to a model with a Save characteristic of 3+ or better, that attack has a Damage characteristic of 2.
Heavy phosphor blaster	36"	Heavy 3	6	-2	1	Each time an attack is made with this weapon, the target does not receive the benefits of Dense Cover against that attack.
Incendine combustor	12"	Heavy D6	5	-2	1	Each time an attack is made with this weapon, that attack automatically hits the target.
Kastelan phosphor blaster	24"	Heavy 3	6	-1	2	Each time an attack is made with this weapon, the target does not receive the benefits of Dense Cover against that attack.
Kataphron plasma culverin		Before selecting targets, select one of the profiles below to make attacks with.				
- Standard	36"	Heavy D6	7	-3	1	Blast
- Supercharge	36"	Heavy D6	8	-3	2	Blast. Each time an unmodified hit roll of 1 is made for an attack with this weapon profile, the bearer's unit suffers 1 mortal wound after shooting with this weapon.
Macrostubber	12"	Pistol 5	4	0	1	-
Magnarail lance	36"	Heavy 1	7	-3	3	-
Mechanicus pistol	12"	Pistol 2	4	-2	1	-
Multi-melta	24"	Heavy 2	8	-4	D6	Each time an attack made with this weapon targets a unit within half range, that attack has a Damage characteristic of D6+2.
Neutron laser	48"	Heavy D3	12	-4	D3+3	Blast
Phosphor blast carbine	18"	Assault 2D3	5	-1	1	Blast. Each time an attack is made with this weapon, the target does not receive the benefits of Dense Cover against that attack.
Phosphor blast pistol	12"	Pistol D3	5	-1	1	Blast. Each time an attack is made with this weapon, the target does not receive the benefits of Dense Cover against that attack.
Phosphor blaster	24"	Rapid Fire 1	5	-1	1	Each time an attack is made with this weapon, the target does not receive the benefits of Dense Cover against that attack.
Phosphor pistol	12"	Pistol 1	4	-1	1	Each time an attack is made with this weapon, the target does not receive the benefits of Dense Cover against that attack.
Phosphor serpenta	18"	Assault 1	5	-1	1	Each time an attack is made with this weapon, the target does not receive the benefits of Dense Cover against that attack.
Phosphor torch	12"	Assault D6	4	-1	1	Each time an attack is made with this weapon, that attack automatically hits the target.
Plasma caliver		Before selecting targets, select one of the profiles below to make attacks with.				
- Standard	30"	Assault 2	7	-3	1	-
- Supercharge	30"	Assault 2	8	-3	2	If any unmodified hit rolls of 1 are made for attacks with this weapon profile, the bearer is destroyed after shooting with this weapon.
Plasma cannon		Before selecting targets, select one of the profiles below to make attacks with.				
- Standard	36"	Heavy D3	7	-3	1	Blast
- Supercharge	36"	Heavy D3	8	-3	2	Blast. If any unmodified hit rolls of 1 are made for attacks with this weapon profile, the bearer is destroyed after shooting with this weapon.
Radium carbine	18"	Assault 3	3	0	1	Each time an attack is made with this weapon against an enemy unit (excluding **VEHICLE** units), an unmodified hit roll of 6 automatically wounds the target.
Radium jezzail	30"	Heavy 2	5	-2	1	Each time you select a target for this weapon, you can ignore the Look Out, Sir rule. Each time an attack is made with this weapon against an enemy unit (excluding **VEHICLE** units), an unmodified hit roll of 6 automatically wounds the target.
Radium pistol	12"	Pistol 1	3	0	1	Each time an attack is made with this weapon against an enemy unit (excluding **VEHICLE** units), an unmodified hit roll of 6 automatically wounds the target.
Radium serpenta	18"	Assault 1	3	0	1	Each time an attack is made with this weapon against an enemy unit (excluding **VEHICLE** units), an unmodified hit roll of 6 automatically wounds the target.
Solar atomiser	12"	Assault D3	10	-4	3	Blast. Each time an attack made with this weapon targets a unit within half range, that attack has a Damage characteristic of D3+3.
Stubcarbine	18"	Pistol 3	4	0	1	-

RANGED WEAPONS	RANGE	TYPE	S	AP	D	ABILITIES
Sulphur breath	12"	Pistol D6	4	-2	1	Each time an attack is made with this weapon, that attack automatically hits the target.
Torsion cannon	48"	Heavy 1	8	-4	D3+3	-
Transonic cannon	12"	Assault D6	4	-1	2	Each time an attack is made with this weapon, that attack automatically hits the target. Each time an attack is made with this weapon, an unmodified wound roll of 6 inflicts 1 mortal wound on the target in addition to any normal damage.
Transuranic arquebus	60"	Heavy 1	7	-2	D3	Each time you select a target for this weapon, you can ignore the Look Out, Sir rule. Each time an attack is made with this weapon, an unmodified wound roll of 6 inflicts 1 mortal wound on the target in addition to any normal damage.
Twin cognis autocannon	48"	Assault 6	7	-1	2	-
Twin cognis heavy stubber	36"	Assault 8	4	0	1	-
Twin cognis lascannon	48"	Assault 2	9	-3	D3+3	-
Twin Icarus autocannon	48"	Heavy 4	7	-1	2	Each time an attack is made with this weapon profile against an **AIRCRAFT** unit, add 1 to that attack's hit roll.
Twin Onager heavy phosphor blaster	36"	Heavy 8	6	-2	2	Each time an attack is made with this weapon, the target does not receive the benefits of Dense Cover against that attack.
Volkite blaster	24"	Heavy 3	6	0	2	Each time an attack is made with this weapon, an unmodified wound roll of 6 inflicts 2 mortal wounds on the target in addition to any normal damage.

114

MELEE WEAPONS	RANGE	TYPE	S	AP	D	ABILITIES
Arc claw	Melee	Melee	+1	-3	1	Each time the bearer fights, it makes 1 additional attack with this weapon. Each time an attack is made with this weapon against a **VEHICLE** unit, that attack has a Damage characteristic of 2 and an unmodified wound roll of 4+ successfully wounds the target.
Arc maul	Melee	Melee	+3	-2	1	Each time an attack is made with this weapon against a **VEHICLE** unit, that attack has a Damage characteristic of 2 and an unmodified wound roll of 4+ successfully wounds the target.
Arc scourge	Melee	Melee	x2	-2	1	Each time an attack is made with this weapon against a **VEHICLE** unit, that attack has a Damage characteristic of 2 and an unmodified wound roll of 2+ successfully wounds the target.
Cavalry sabre	Melee	Melee	+1	-1	1	-
Chordclaw	Melee	Melee	User	-1	1	Each time the bearer fights, it makes 1 additional attack with this weapon.
Clawed limbs	Melee	Melee	+1	0	1	Each time the bearer fights, it makes 2 additional attacks with this weapon.
Control stave	Melee	Melee	+3	-2	1	-
Electroleech stave	Melee	Melee	+2	-2	2	Each time an attack is made with this weapon, an unmodified wound roll of 6 inflicts 2 mortal wounds on the target and the attack sequence ends.
Electrostatic gauntlets (melee)	Melee	Melee	+2	-1	1	Each time an attack is made with this weapon, an unmodified hit roll of 6 scores 2 additional hits.
Hydraulic claw	Melee	Melee	x2	-2	3	-
Kastelan fist	Melee	Melee	+4	-3	3	Each time the bearer fights, it makes 1 additional attack with this weapon.
Manipulus mechadendrites	Melee	Melee	User	0	1	Each time the bearer fights, it makes 3 additional attacks with this weapon.
Mechadendrite hive	Melee	Melee	User	0	1	Each time the bearer fights, it makes 2D6 additional attacks with this weapon.
Omnissian axe	Melee	Melee	+2	-2	2	-
Omnissian staff	Melee	Melee	+3	-1	2	-
Power fist	Melee	Melee	x2	-3	2	Each time an attack is made with this weapon, subtract 1 from that attack's hit roll.
Power sword	Melee	Melee	+1	-3	1	-
Pteraxii talons	Melee	Melee	User	-1	1	-
Servo-arc claw	Melee	Melee	+3	-2	3	Each time the bearer fights, no more than one attack can be made with each servo-arc claw. Each time an attack is made with this weapon against a **VEHICLE** unit, that attack has a Damage characteristic of 4 and an unmodified wound roll of 4+ successfully wounds the target.
Servo-arm	Melee	Melee	x2	-2	3	Each time the bearer fights, no more than one attack can be made with each servo-arm.
Taser goad	Melee	Melee	+2	-1	1	Each time an attack is made with this weapon, an unmodified hit roll of 6 scores 2 additional hits.
Taser lance	Melee	Melee	+3	-2	2	Each time an attack is made with this weapon, an unmodified hit roll of 6 scores 2 additional hits.
Transonic blades	Melee	Melee	+1	-3	1	Each time an attack is made with this weapon, an unmodified wound roll of 6 inflicts 1 mortal wound on the target in addition to any normal damage.
Transonic razor	Melee	Melee	User	-2	1	Each time an attack is made with this weapon, an unmodified wound roll of 6 inflicts 1 mortal wound on the target in addition to any normal damage.

POINTS VALUES

You can use this section to determine the points (pts) value of each unit in your army. Each entry lists the unit's size (i.e. how many models the unit can contain) and how many points the unit costs. If an entry has a unit cost of 'x pts/model', then the unit costs *x* points for every model in that unit. You must then add points for each weapon, or item of wargear, that is included in that unit if it is listed in that unit's entry (weapons and other wargear not listed in a unit's entry cost no additional points to include in that unit).

 HQ

Belisarius Cawl (pg 86)
Unit size ....1 model
Unit cost.................................. 180 pts

Skitarii Marshal (pg 90)
Unit size ....1 model
Unit cost.....................................45 pts

Tech-Priest Dominus (pg 88)
Unit size ....1 model
Unit cost.....................................75 pts
- Eradication ray ....+5 pts
- Phosphor serpenta ....+5 pts

Tech-Priest Enginseer (pg 91)
Unit size ....1 model
Unit cost.....................................55 pts

Tech-Priest Manipulus (pg 87)
Unit size ....1 model
Unit cost.....................................70 pts
- Transonic cannon ....+5 pts

Technoarcheologist (pg 89)
Unit size ....1 model
Unit cost.....................................55 pts

Holy Orders (pg 64-65)
- Genetors.....................................25 pts
- Logi ....35 pts
- Magi ....30 pts
- Artisans ....25 pts

▶ TROOPS

Kataphron Breachers (pg 94)
Unit size .... 3-6 models
Unit cost.............................35 pts/model
- Torsion cannon ....+10 pts

Kataphron Destroyers (pg 95)
Unit size .... 3-6 models
Unit cost.............................40 pts/model
- Cognis flamer ....+5 pts
- Kataphron plasma culverin...............+10 pts

Skitarii Rangers (pg 92)
Unit size ....5-20 models
Unit cost................................ 8 pts/model
- Arc maul....................................+5 pts
- Arc pistol..................................+5 pts
- Arc rifle ....+10 pts
- Enhanced data-tether ....+5 pts
- Omnispex...................................+5 pts
- Phosphor blast pistol.................+5 pts
- Plasma caliver ....+10 pts
- Power sword.............................+5 pts
- Taser goad.................................+5 pts
- Transuranic arquebus.........................+15 pts

Skitarii Vanguard (pg 93)
Unit size ....5-20 models
Unit cost................................ 8 pts/model
- Arc maul....................................+5 pts
- Arc pistol..................................+5 pts
- Arc rifle ....+10 pts
- Enhanced data-tether ....+5 pts
- Omnispex...................................+5 pts
- Phosphor blast pistol.................+5 pts
- Plasma caliver ....+10 pts
- Power sword.............................+5 pts
- Taser goad.................................+5 pts
- Transuranic arquebus.........................+15 pts

✠ ELITES

Corpuscarii Electro-Priests (pg 97)
Unit size ....5-20 models
Unit cost.............................15 pts/model

Cybernetica Datasmith (pg 98)
Unit size ....1 model
Unit cost.....................................40 pts

Fulgurite Electro-Priests (pg 97)
Unit size ....5-20 models
Unit cost.............................15 pts/model

Servitors (pg 96)
Unit size .... 4 models
Unit cost.....................................28 pts
- Heavy bolter.............................+10 pts
- Multi-melta ....+20 pts
- Plasma cannon.........................+15 pts

Sicarian Infiltrators (pg 98)
Unit size ....5-10 models
Unit cost.............................17 pts/model

Sicarian Ruststalkers (pg 99)
Unit size ....5-10 models
Unit cost.............................17 pts/model

⚡ FAST ATTACK

Ironstrider Ballistarii (pg 103)
Unit size ....1-6 models
Unit cost..65 pts/model
- Twin cognis lascannon ....+10 pts

Pteraxii Skystalkers (pg 103)
Unit size ....5-10 models
Unit cost..17 pts/model

Pteraxii Sterylizors (pg 102)
Unit size ....5-10 models
Unit cost..19 pts/model

Serberys Raiders (pg 100)
Unit size ....3-9 models
Unit cost..16 pts/model
- Enhanced data-tether ....+5 pts

Serberys Sulphurhounds (pg 101)
Unit size ....3-9 models
Unit cost..20 pts/model
- Arc maul..+5 pts
- Phosphor blast carbine ....+10 pts
- Phosphor blast pistol..............................+5 pts

Sydonian Dragoons (pg 104)
Unit size ....1-6 models
Unit cost..55 pts/model
- Phosphor serpenta...................................+5 pts
- Taser lance..+15 pts

👑 HEAVY SUPPORT

Kastelan Robots (pg 105)
Unit size .... 2-6 models
Unit cost.. 100 pts/model
- Kastelan phosphor blaster ....+5 pts

Onager Dunecrawler (pg 107)
Unit size ....1 model
Unit cost.. 115 pts
- Cognis heavy stubber.............................+5 pts

Skorpius Disintegrator (pg 106)
Unit size ....1 model
Unit cost.. 145 pts

☠ DEDICATED TRANSPORTS

Skorpius Dunerider (pg 108)
Unit size ....1 model
Unit cost.*.. 95 pts

🌿 FLYERS

Archaeopter Fusilave (pg 111)
Unit size ....1 model
Unit cost.. 130 pts
- Chaff launcher ....+20 pts

Archaeopter Stratoraptor (pg 110)
Unit size ....1 model
Unit cost.. 160 pts
- Chaff launcher ....+20 pts

Archaeopter Transvector (pg 109)
Unit size ....1 model
Unit cost.. 110 pts
- Chaff launcher ....+20 pts

GLOSSARY

Below you will find a glossary that contains a number of terms used in this Codex.

Adeptus Mechanicus Detachment (pg 49): A Detachment in a Battle-forged army where every model has the **Adeptus Mechanicus** keyword (excluding models with the **Agent of the Imperium** or **Unaligned** keywords).

Adeptus Mechanicus secondary objectives (pg 70): Additional secondary objectives that can be used in certain matched play mission packs, if every Detachment in your army is an **Adeptus Mechanicus** Detachment.

Any number of models can each have their Weapon A replaced with Weapon B: When this wargear option is selected for a unit, any number of models in that unit that are equipped with Weapon A can each have its weapon replaced with Weapon B. It is possible for only some of the models in that unit to have their weapon replaced and for others not to.

Arc weapon (pg 112): A weapon whose profile includes the word 'arc', or a Relic that replaces an arc weapon.

Arcana Mechanicum (pg 68-69): A type of Relic that can be given to **Adeptus Mechanicus Character** models.

Archeotech force field (pg 78-81): In Crusade, a piece of wargear carried by **Tech-Priest** models, created by assembling a power source and a force field part together.

Archeotech techno-arcana (pg 78-81): In Crusade, a piece of wargear carried by **Tech-Priest** models, created by assembling a power source and a techno-arcana part together.

Archeotech weapon (pg 78-81): In Crusade, a weapon carried by **Tech-Priest** models, created by assembling a power source and a weapon part together.

Carbine weapon (pg 112): A ranged weapon whose profile includes the word 'carbine', or a Relic that replaces a carbine weapon.

Cognis weapon (pg 112): A ranged weapon whose profile includes the word 'cognis', or a Relic that replaces a cognis weapon.

Force Field part (pg 80): In Crusade, an archeotech part that can be found and combined with other archeotech parts.

Forge World (pg 84): Adeptus Mechanicus units with the **<Forge World>** keyword will belong to one Forge World. When you include such a unit in your army, you must select a Forge World's keyword to replace this keyword with.

Forge World Arcana Mechanicum (pg 50): An Arcana Mechanicum associated with a specific Forge World. These are only available to **Character** models that are part of a Forge World Detachment (and only if they, and your Warlord, are drawn from the associated Forge World).

Forge World Detachment (pg 50): An **Adeptus Mechanicus** Detachment in which every **Adeptus Mechanicus** unit that is from a Forge World is from the same Forge World.

Forge World Dogmas (pg 49): Detachment ability for **Adeptus Mechanicus** Detachments.

Forge World Warlord Trait (pg 50): A Warlord Trait associated with a specific Forge World. These are only available to **Warlords** that are part of a Forge World Detachment (and only if they are from the associated Forge World).

From: The Forge World that a unit belongs to is the Forge World they are from. A unit is from a certain Forge World if they have that Forge World's name listed on its Faction keyword line.

Galvanic weapon (pg 112): A ranged weapon whose profile includes the word 'galvanic', or a Relic that replaces a galvanic weapon.

Holy Orders (pg 64-65): A unique upgrade that can be given to **Adeptus Mechanicus Tech-Priest** models (excluding named characters).

Phosphor weapon (pg 112): A ranged weapon whose profile includes the word 'phosphor', or a Relic that replaces a phosphor weapon.

Plasma weapon (pg 112): A ranged weapon whose profile includes the word 'plasma', or a Relic that replaces a plasma weapon.

Power Source (pg 79): In Crusade, an archeotech part that can be found and combined with other archeotech parts.

Questor Mechanicus Detachment: A Detachment in a Battle-forged army where every model has the **Questor Mechanicus** keyword (excluding models with the **Agent of the Imperium** or **Unaligned** keywords).

Radium weapon (pg 112): A ranged weapon whose profile includes the word 'radium', or a Relic that replaces a radium weapon.

Rifle weapon (pg 112): A ranged weapon whose profile includes the word 'rifle', or a Relic that replaces a rifle weapon.

Stratagem label: A Stratagem's labels are written beneath its title and can include: Adeptus Mechanicus; Battle Tactic; Epic Deed, Strategic Ploy; Requisition; Wargear. A Stratagem can have more than one label; for example, a Stratagem with 'Adeptus Mechanicus – Wargear Stratagem' has both the Adeptus Mechanicus and Wargear labels.

Taser weapon (pg 112): A melee weapon whose profile includes the word 'taser', or a Relic that replaces a taser weapon.

Techno-arcana part (pg 81): In Crusade, an archeotech part that can be found and combined with other archeotech parts.

Weapon part (pg 80): In Crusade, an archeotech part that can be found and combined with other archeotech parts.

REFERENCE

Below you will find a bullet-pointed summary of several Adeptus Mechanicus rules.

<FORGE WORLD> KEYWORD (PG 84)

- When you include a unit with the **<FORGE WORLD>** keyword, nominate which Forge World it is from.
- Replace every instance of the **<FORGE WORLD>** keyword on that unit's datasheet with the name of your chosen Forge World.

ARCHEOTECH (PG 78-81)

- In Crusade, your force acquires pieces of archeotech. Each piece of archeotech is one of the following: power source; force-field part; techno-arcana part; weapon part.
- One power source is combined with one of the other pieces of archeotech to make a new piece of wargear.
- **TECH-PRIEST** models can be equipped with these wargear items when mustering your army.

CANTICLES OF THE OMNISSIAH (PG 84-85)

- Canticles of the Omnissiah only applies if every model in your army has the **ADEPTUS MECHANICUS** keyword (excluding **AGENT OF THE IMPERIUM, KNIGHT OF THE COG** and **UNALIGNED** models).
- At the start of the battle round, select one Canticle that you have not yet selected this game.
- Until the end of the battle round, models with this ability gain a new ability based on the Canticle that was selected.

DOCTRINA IMPERATIVES (PG 84-85)

- Doctrina Imperatives only applies if every model in your army has the **ADEPTUS MECHANICUS** keyword (excluding **AGENT OF THE IMPERIUM, KNIGHT OF THE COG** and **UNALIGNED** models).
- Imperatives have two parts: an Optimised effect, which improves a model's characteristics, and a Deprecated effect, which reduces a model's characteristics.
- At the start of the battle round, if a **DOCTRINA ASSEMBLER** model from your army is on the battlefield, you can select one Imperative that you have not yet selected this game.
- If an Imperative is selected, until the end of the battle round, models with this ability have their characteristics modified by both that Imperative's Optimised and its Deprecated effects.

DETACHMENT ABILITIES (PG 49)

- If your army is Battle-forged, **ADEPTUS MECHANICUS** Detachments gain Forge World Dogmas and Knight of the Cog abilities.
- If your army is Battle-forged, Troops units in **ADEPTUS MECHANICUS** Detachments gain the Objective Secured ability (see Warhammer 40,000 Core Book).
- This does not apply to Auxiliary Support, Super-heavy Auxiliary, or Fortification Network Detachments.

FORGE WORLD DOGMAS (PG 49-59)

- If every unit in a Detachment is drawn from the same Forge World, all **ADEPTUS MECHANICUS** units in that Detachment gain a dogma.
- THe dogma gained depends on what Forge World they are from.
- If a Forge World does not have an associated dogma, you must create one for them. To do so, select one Primary and one of its associated Secondaries from pages 58-59.

HOLY ORDERS (PG 64-65)

- If your army is Battle-forged, you can upgrade **TECH-PRIEST** models.
- Doing so increases a model's Power Rating and points value.
- The upgraded model will gain two new abilities, one of which is a progressive ability.
- Your army cannot contain more than one model with the same upgrade.
- Crusade armies must use the Holy Orders Requisition to upgrade characters.
- You cannot upgrade named characters.

KNIGHT OF THE COG (PG 49)

- If your army is Battle-forged, for each Detachment with this ability, select one **QUESTOR MECHANICUS** Super-heavy Auxiliary Detachment.
- Units in the selected Detachment gain the **KNIGHT OF THE COG** keyword.

PROGRESSIVE ABILITY (PG 64-65)

- This ability has two parts, Initial and Advanced.
- A model starts with the Initial part active, while the Advanced part does nothing.
- A model can use an action to make the Advanced part active, and the Initial part then does nothing.